Crying at the Movies

D1374245

Crying

AT THE

MOVIES

A Film Memoir

MADELON SPRENGNETHER

Graywolf Press
SAINT PAUL, MINNESOTA

Publication of this volume is made possible in part by a grant provided by the Minnesota State Arts Board, through an appropriation by the Minnesota State Legislature, a grant from the Wells Fargo Foundation Minnesota, and a grant from the National Endowment for the Arts. Significant support has also been provided by the Bush Foundation; Marshall Field's Project Imagine with support from Target Foundation; the McKnight Foundation; and other generous contributions from foundations, corporations, and individuals. To these organizations and individuals we offer our heartfelt thanks.

Special funding for this title has been provided by the Jerome Foundation.

"Shadow Love" first appeared in *Womens Studies* under the title "Afterlife." Copyright © 2001 by Overseas Publishers Association N.V. Reprinted with permission from Taylor & Francis Ltd.
"Ponte Dell' Abbadia (Vulci)," from the poem "Etruscan Pages" by Kathleen Fraser. Reprinted from *il cuore: the heart: Selected Poems: 1970–1995*, copyright © 1997 by Kathleen Fraser, with the permission of Wesleyan University Press.
"The Wild Iris," copyright © 1992 by Louise Glück. Reprinted from *The Wild Iris* with the permission of The Ecco Press.
Excerpts from *The Piano* by Jane Campion. Hyperion (Miramax Books), 1993.

Published by Graywolf Press
2402 University Avenue, Suite 203
Saint Paul, Minnesota 55114
All rights reserved.

www.graywolfpress.org

Published in the United States of America
Printed in Canada

ISBN 1-55597-358-2

2 4 6 8 9 7 5 3 1
First Graywolf Printing, 2002

Library of Congress Control Number: 2001088679

Cover design: Scott Sorenson

CONTENTS

For Jessica

Have you noticed that only in time of illness
or disaster or death are people real?

     — Walker Percy, *The Moviegoer*

Mourning is the other face of loving.

     — Alice Koller, *The Stations of Solitude*

Crying at the Movies

Home Movies

I HAVE NO MEMORY of my father's drowning when I was nine years old. I was present at the scene—along with my mother and two brothers—and I can remember things that happened immediately before and after, but I don't recall anything related to the actual moment of his disappearance.

I used to think it was because I was inattentive. Maybe I had my back turned. Or I had my mind on something else. I just didn't notice. But how can this be? How could I have *missed* an event of such significance?

Both of my brothers—one of whom was seven years old at the time, the other twelve—have memories (though they don't completely jibe) of what happened. Only I draw a blank. In the place of narrative, I have only an image. When I force myself to focus on this instant, what I see is a piece of over-exposed film. There was too much light.

I knew I had lost my father, but I somehow missed the *experience* of his loss. The gap in my memory contained the terrifying feelings that flashed through me at the moment of his death. Where did they go? Am I even sure I had them? How to validate the existence of something you simply can't remember? Trauma, I have since learned, can induce this kind of amnesia. In trauma, the self is overwhelmed. Faced with the imminent threat of annihilation, it blinks, steps aside, opts out. What is not perceived, in turn, seems not to exist. Trauma, according to the psychoanalytic theorist Cathy Caruth, causes "a break in the mind's experience of time," the shock of which causes a temporary blank.

Yet, even if I could, through hypnosis or some other

means, recover a semblance of memory of my father's drowning, what would it tell me? Not much more, I think, than what I already know. That there was a violent rupture in my sense of reality, a dividing of my life into "before" and "after," and a consequent deadening of my capacity to feel—not just grief or sorrow, but also (more significantly and tragically) love.

My emotions, like migrating birds, fled the cold climate of my heart, alighting somewhere else, where, from a safe distance, I could sometimes view them. This was the function of reading, for me, in childhood. I devoured tales of orphans and sick or dying girls—books like *Heidi, Little Women,* and *The Secret Garden.* I couldn't get enough of such books, though I also didn't understand the source of my appetite. Eventually, this habit led me to a Ph.D. in English literature.

Yet the first time I truly encountered one of my lost and alienated selves was not in the solitude of my study poring over a novel of traumatic orphanhood, like *Bleak House* or *Jane Eyre,* but at the movies. I first wept, in a desperate and brokenhearted way, not over a loss of my own but that of someone whom I did not know, who didn't actually exist, and who belonged to a radically different culture. I had this sudden emotional breakdown at the age of twenty-six, while watching the classic Indian film *Pather Panchali,* by director Satyajit Ray. I wasn't merely tearful, I was convulsed. My crying was totally physical and out of my control. While the film deals with death, I had seen plenty of movies about death without having a reaction like this. Why this story, in particular, and why now?

For years afterward, I cried at the movies. When bad things happened to me in real life, I didn't react. I seemed cool or indifferent. Yet in the dark and relative safety of the movie theater, I would weep over fictional tragedies, over someone else's suffering. So deeply ingrained was this habit that I didn't think to question it until my convulsive reaction to *Pather Panchali* surfaced again in my mid-fifties—in a dramatic and ultimately life-changing way.

I was watching Peter Weir's *Fearless,* a film about the aftermath of an airplane crash. The hero, a survivor of the crash, suffers flashbacks throughout the film, but it is only at the end that his memory of the experience fully unfolds. In the midst of this sequence, which takes place in slow motion to the accompaniment of a somber musical score, I started to cry. Once I had started, I couldn't stop, seized by the same inexplicable force that had overtaken me while watching *Pather Panchali,* nearly twenty-five years earlier.

My husband Robert, who was sitting next to me, held my shoulders and tried to comfort me, but he didn't say anything. Neither of us talked about it afterward. I couldn't find the words to express what I felt, and Robert didn't ask. It was as though we had agreed to forget the whole incident. Several months later, we had a violent argument over the movie *Schindler's List.*

All winter we had been separated by our academic jobs. He was in Chicago on a research leave, while I was in Minneapolis administering a creative writing program. We saw each other every third weekend. In between these moments of respite, I entertained myself by going to movies alone. Without intending to, I found myself seeing a series of movies that made me cry: *The Piano, Philadelphia,* and *Shadowlands.* When *Schindler's List* came out, I knew I wanted to see it, but was afraid of going by myself. Robert and I talked about seeing it together, but the movie was so long that our timing was usually off. Finally, it looked as though we could make it. To my surprise, Robert resisted. He had been reading reviews that described some especially violent scenes. "I don't want to see this," he said bluntly. "I know about the Holocaust already. I don't need to watch a woman get shot with a pistol, point-blank in the head."

I was taken off guard. Because I had counted on Robert's company, I took his refusal personally. I thought he understood how much I needed him to go with me and couldn't understand his sudden display of insensitivity. He couldn't understand why I was upset. "It's only a movie," he kept insisting, at first with bewilderment and finally with exasperation. Eventually, he became angry and for a while stopped speaking to me.

What my husband didn't know—and what I was unable to convey to him—was that I was anxious about having another movie-theater breakdown. I expected *Schindler's List* to be so sad that I would cry the way I did at *Fearless*. I was afraid of being alone with so much sadness.

Robert and I never resolved our argument that day. We treated it the way we did my crying over *Fearless*; we didn't talk about it. Not long afterward, I slipped into a romantic involvement with someone else.

I'm not good at deception, and after three weeks of this relationship, I confessed. My husband was understandably angry and hurt. We did the usual things; we went into counseling, talked, fought, withdrew, made love. Neither of us had a clue. Finally, after four months of exhausting effort, Robert felt he could not go on in this way. He came home from work one day and told me he had filed for divorce. "When," he demanded, "can you move out?"

This was my second marriage, and I had expected it to last to the end of my days. When it terminated abruptly in my mid-fifties, I had to ask myself what had gone wrong. I had been happy—so I thought—yet I did something I could not account for. My affair was not just an ordinary dalliance, but an entanglement that shook my confidence in myself.

Twenty years before, my first marriage had broken off in a similar manner. While the circumstances were different, the underlying pattern was the same. I had an affair that dealt a fatal blow to my marriage. This realization unnerved me. Had nothing changed?

Twice I have had a love relationship so involving and intense as to throw my whole life into upheaval. Each time I have surprised myself—as though someone I didn't know were acting in my place. Who is this wild woman, I wondered, and why is she doing these things? My exploration of these questions led me to re-examine the impact of my father's sudden, accidental death in the summer of 1951—an event that not only traumatized me as a child and shaped my growing up, but cast a shadow of unresolved mourning over my adult life.

My father drowned in the Mississippi River, on a family boat trip, somewhere above St. Louis. We owned a cabin cruiser, which my dad loved and which we used at every opportunity for weekend outings and more extended vacations. It was the end of summer, the Labor Day weekend. Although we often took excursions with friends, anchoring off a sandbar for swimming, beach fires, and barbecues, this time we were alone. We had stopped sometime mid-afternoon. My older brother Bob was showing my father the new swimming strokes he had learned at the neighborhood YMCA, when he was suddenly carried out of his depth. He cried for help. My dad went to rescue him, pushing him toward shore, where my mother waded in to pull him out. In the midst of this confusion, my father himself suddenly vanished. His body was not found for two days.

During this interval, I didn't know what to think. The last thing I wanted to believe was that he was dead. I don't remember crying, nor do I remember anyone confirming for me the fact of his death. Perhaps I have eclipsed such memories in the same way that I effaced the actual moment of his disappearance. The result, however, is the same. Everything about the aftermath of my father's death seemed unreal. Time was no longer seamless, but double. One part of me lived in a present devoid of animation, while another remained locked in the past, flash frozen into place by the shock of my father's departure. This part, which also bore the burden of my emotions, was as lost to me as my conscious memory of that moment. As a consequence, I was not able to mourn. I suspect that the same holds true for my mother and two brothers. Instead, we stumbled toward the future, dazed by our loss.

The trauma of my father's death was such that it prevented us from grieving. Yet grief that is not felt or acknowledged does not dissipate; it goes underground, where it flourishes, like some evil plant, in secret and debilitating ways. Sometimes it sickens the mind, sometimes the body. Occasionally, it infects both.

The strategy I devised to cope with a world suddenly deprived of safety and comfort was improvised out of desperation; I developed an unnatural passivity. Being a quiet child already, I became even more watchful, obedient, and submissive. Having a disposition toward rheumatic fever (which I had suffered twice in a mild form before my father died), I succumbed to a third, more virulent bout. What I relinquished in the aftermath of my father's death was resilience. I lost faith in myself. What I had left (an inquiring mind and a desire to be good) was limited—just enough to get me through childhood and adolescence. But not enough to flourish as an adult.

Three years after my second marriage broke up, I decided to read my journals from this time, including the months preceding the argument over *Schindler's List*. What I discovered in this mountain of material was a double narrative—one describing the powerful feelings of sadness that certain films evoked, the other documenting the disintegration of my marriage. Neither made sense alone, but both acquired meaning when viewed as part of a process of deferred mourning.

My breakdown over *Pather Panchali* formed the template for many such experiences, all of which were keyed to my suppressed emotions. What I could see or react to on the screen, I could not feel in everyday life—except in the context of a life-altering affair.

Crying at the movies, I have come to understand, was a way for me to begin to feel the pain of my father's death. The loss I could not acknowledge in my own life I could recognize and react to onscreen. It was as though the sadness I had buried when I was nine years old lay deep within my psyche, waiting for its shadow image to appear in the dreamlike space of the movie theater. Each time this occurred, I felt seized by an emotion I could not control. I cried helplessly and shamelessly, as if I were an actor in the drama unfolding before my eyes. Having a disastrous love affair at two significant moments in my life translated these passionate feelings into reality. At these times, I experienced the pain and sorrow I was too frightened to feel as a child.

But what is it about movies? Why should I begin to recover through this medium? Why not music, painting, sculpture, dance? Or literature, my chosen field?

There are some obvious answers. The movie theater is a special environment, a liminal space, between dream and reality, where anything seems possible. It is a twilight zone, a place where we can be suddenly assaulted—or enlightened— by the shock of the unfamiliar. Stories and fantasies we normally labor to suppress or forget appear, writ large, before our eyes in Dolby sound and full-screen Technicolor. The movie theater is just safe—and just scary—enough to breach our ordinary defenses, permitting a relaxation of the boundary between conscious and unconscious awareness.

For adults, the movie theater also recreates the world of play we once knew as children—where we could act out the full range of our wishes and impulses, without fear or consequence. Many of us give ourselves up to this experience, relinquishing our mundane identities, our composure, even our sense of interior inviolability.

Yet these are general explanations—ones that apply to nearly everyone. How to explain my particular and radical vulnerability to film? While I don't have a definitive answer to this question, I suspect that one may be found in the primary documentary record of my childhood before my father's death—our family home movies.

My dad was the photographer and filmmaker in our family. It was he who took the black-and-white snapshots, which (still unsorted) fill a drawer in my mother's house, and he who shot the miscellaneous reels of color film that show us awkwardly, shyly, but also spontaneously, in motion. For years, these films lay stored in a cabinet my mother never opened. I used to sneak a look at them when I visited her—as if, like Superman, I could penetrate their opaque tin canisters for a glimpse of my past, that hidden and inaccessible treasure. I was well into my forties before I was able to summon the courage to ask if it was all right to view them.

What happened when I did was heart stopping. Unfolding before my eyes, I saw the family we had been—playful, laughing, preening, mugging—wide open and completely unprepared for the tragedy that awaited us. We couldn't have been more vulnerable. The way my mother's face lit up when she turned to face my dad, the way my brothers and I broke up over his jokes—these things were not the product of directorial control. My father filmed what he loved, and what he loved was us.

Other things he loved: flowing water, shorelines and

beaches, especially the Mississippi River; boats of any kind, speedboats, sailboats, paddleboats, our own cabin cruiser named "Sinbad" for the fictional wanderer and adventurer; flying, including the panoramic views of mountains, craters, and chasms afforded by such; his business, manufacturing seismographs, those delicate devices for sensing the smallest oscillations of the earth; good times, drinking beer, or eating barbecue with his family and friends.

Watching these movies—despite the fact that my father was mostly behind, rather than in front of, the camera—was the clearest way for me to remember him. It wasn't his image that I needed to recover, but something about his perfume or flavor, his sensibility.

One sequence is especially meaningful to me. Now transferred to video, the multiple, short reels are jumbled chronologically, but they end in a way that I can only describe as symbolic. Whether by accident or design, the tape concludes with my parents' trip to Hawaii (a business-combined-with-pleasure jaunt) in November of 1950—a mere nine months before my father's death.

My dad begins by outlining his trip—which included Australia and New Zealand, where he installed seismograph stations, after my mother returned home from Hawaii—by turning an enormous globe and pointing to his farthest destination. Then there are scenes shot from behind the wing of a propeller airplane: some badlands, a crater, the basin and range territory of the West, followed by a view from the ground, with scrub brush on either side of the road and steam rising from volcanic "hot spots" deep within the earth's crust. My dad made a living from studying the signs of the earth's inherent instability and volatility.

The scenes from Hawaii are idyllic. My mom and dad in leis and Hawaiian shirts appear in a variety of exotic settings—in front of the Royal Hawaiian Hotel in Honolulu—

next to a lily pond at a restaurant—in front of a banyan tree—
on a sailboat—on a catamaran—in a convertible on a road
into the mountains, flanked by pineapple fields—walking
into a cave—on the beach. My dad, in shorts and a palm-
frond hat, chops a bunch of bananas from a tree. My mother,
in a swimming suit, shakes her loosened, waist-length hair
in front of her face. My beautiful, young parents seem to be
having the time of their lives.

There is one lovely sequence that encapsulates this moment for me in its poignance and fragility. A Hawaiian
woman, dressed in a long, dark muumuu with a pink flower
design, performs a hula dance in slow motion. She is bare-
foot, wears an orchid lei, and has a large, red hibiscus tucked
behind one ear. She dances on the grass in front of a stand of
rosebushes, which begin to sway from an invisible wind as
she performs. The film is as silent as her story, which she
tells, over and over again, in a complex choreography, the
meaning of which I can only guess at.

There is a departure and a call. Her hips sway. She turns
her head to the left and then to the right. One hand flutters,
in a descending motion, next to her mouth. I can't tell
whether this is a tale of fidelity, reunion, or loss. The only
thing I know is that my dad, who filmed it, couldn't take
his eyes off of this story. The film speed deliberately slows—
the roses in the background drifting first one way, then
another—as if to retard the relentless passage of time.

After my father left Hawaii to continue his business trip,
he filmed mostly landscapes: lakes and mountains viewed
from a seaplane; an observatory, a city with trams, bagpipers
in a street parade, and men playing cricket and bowls; a
Maori village with thatched houses and red, carved wood
totem figures with bright abalone shells for eyes; a geyser
shooting like "Old Faithful" out of the rocky ground; kanga-
roos and peacocks in a zoo, sheep in a pasture and a long,
cascading waterfall. At the end, he stands next to a giant

replica of the globe he has navigated, tracing with his forefinger the trajectory of his trip—from St. Louis to California,
to Hawaii, to Australia, to New Zealand and back. He is
wearing a white lab coat in this scene, and we see only his
arm—not his face.

There is something magisterial in this gesture, as if my father owned the earth he spins beneath his fingers. For a moment, he seems omniscient and omnipotent—my child's-eye
view of God. The little world he created on film was his to
shape and manipulate. Perhaps he even shared the scientist's
dream of divining the earth's innermost secrets—the way he
listened to its trembling heart with his finely calibrated in-
struments. I never had a chance to find out. While this movie
attests to an odyssey successfully completed, our modest
family vacation only nine months later was dramatically cut
short. The harbor we set out from at the end of August in 1951
was one we did not return to. I never saw my father again.

I am haunted by a double awareness: on film my father seems
to hold the world in his hands, whereas in reality he was disturbingly mortal. At the movies, I am able to entertain both
of these possibilities. It's as if my dad (like the actual filmmaker or director) were invisibly present somewhere behind
the scenes—while remaining utterly out of reach. In the en-
veloping darkness of the movie theater, I am able to relive
the love and loss I felt as a child, in silent communication
with his ghost.

Film, in a multitude of ways, serves my need to recollect—
to go back and pick up—the feelings I suppressed or abandoned in the process of growing up. I have only been able to
know these feelings, that is to say to live them through and
put them to rest, through a laborious process of displacement and repetition. Slowly, in this way, I have created a
memory where none existed in me before. Not of the event of
my father's death, but of my astonished emotions.

Breaking Down, Breaking Open
1969–1977

Breaking Down, Breaking Open:

Pather Panchali

> (The soundtrack of that film . . . I feared the music
> in retrospect . . . as if it were foretelling everything
> coming toward me . . . paths moving with choral
> inevitability toward all I would love and finally
> lose . . . my own path calling me.)
>
>   — Kathleen Fraser, "Ponte Dell'Abbadia (Vulci)"

Is it possible to be called to one's path by a
movie? Judging from my reaction to *Pather Panchali*, I would
say yes. I went to see this film in January 1969, in a state of
bland indifference, not unlike the smoothly snowbound
landscape of the Vermont town where I was living at the
time. I left the theater sobbing out of control.

It was mid-term of my first year teaching at Middlebury
College, where I had taken a job fresh out of graduate school.
My husband Frank, who wanted to be a photographer and
who was trying to avoid the draft, had come with me to
Vermont, hoping that some combination of his resistance to
the Vietnam War, his depression, and being (just barely)
over age would suffice to relieve him of his I-A status. I was
twenty-six years old, a shy and frightened novice teacher. I
was also six months pregnant.

I am tall, but not very big boned. My body is angular and
tends toward slimness, a combination of genetic heritage
and my childhood history of rheumatic fever with its peri-
odic bouts of loss of appetite. But in January of 1969 I was

round and heavy, so much so that I could barely recognize myself. From the moment of conception, I started gaining weight, my waist thickening, my breasts filling out, my belly pushing ahead of me, hard and insistent. Everything about me, from my ankles to my cheekbones, seemed large and unfamiliar. I hefted this suddenly altered self like a fifty-pound bag of potatoes, the additional weight that I actually carried by the time my daughter was born. Who was I, I wondered, gazing at my pudgy face in the mirror? And who was this creature growing so rapidly and greedily within me?

I had felt out of relation to my body for some years, most likely from the time I first became ill with rheumatic fever at age seven. I began then to view my flesh with distrust, as if it were an alien force bent on thwarting my childish desires—to run, ride my bicycle, jump rope, or play hopscotch. This distrust deepened after my second and third relapses, the last, most prolonged and painful one after my father's death when I was nine. Although I outgrew (or outlived) rheumatic fever, sometime around puberty I began having migraine headaches. Every two weeks or so, I would experience a fuzziness of vision, followed by nausea and blinding pain. Being reassured that my eyesight was OK and that I had no underlying neurological problems, I learned to live with this condition, which usually lasted half a day. Migraines, my doctor said, afflict people with high intelligence and a tendency toward perfectionism. I did not find this description unsettling. Slowly, over a period of years, I became accustomed to ignoring the distress signals of my body, treating them as a distraction or an annoyance, rather than the SOS calls that they were.

I wasn't completely out of touch with my body, just somewhat removed, as if I had two selves, which overlapped but did not fuse, like a double exposure. One part of me stood back, a figure in the shadows who observed but did not fully participate in the activities of the other. Becoming pregnant felt something like this. Although my husband and I made love with regularity and pleasure, I did not immediately connect the lateness of my period or the sudden enlargement and soreness of my breasts with the possibility of conception. I suppose I was feeling invulnerable from having been on the pill for the previous two years, but I think my obliviousness was more deeply ingrained than this. I was simply not used to paying much attention to my physical self.

My body had a surprising new will of its own, inflating me like a hard balloon, changing the way I sat, stood, bent over, walked, and slept, as well as the way I looked. I was ballasted like one of those child's toys with a weight in the bottom. I was sunk, grounded, anchored in my flesh, whether I liked it or not. Some days I would regard my mushrooming body with amazement, wondering also at my voracious appetite. I felt like the snake that swallowed an elephant in Saint-Exupéry's *The Little Prince*.

I read all the childbirth books I could get my hands on, but I still couldn't fathom this transformation in myself. How two could be made of one, in particular how I could accomplish such a radical split. I was both awed and frightened by my body, which I regarded as a huge milkweed pod, timed to rip open, to erupt.

I went to *Pather Panchali* on assignment—as a faculty discussion leader in a team-taught course on film. For me, this course was an education, introducing me to such classics as *Battleship Potemkin, The Cabinet of Dr. Caligari, Un Chien Andalou,* and *La Strada*. I loved this course, eagerly looking forward to each new screening. Our group leader was also fired with enthusiasm. He had us read parts of Freud's *Interpretation of Dreams,* explaining to us how movies are like dreams, making use of similar strategies of condensation and displacement. This was a different way to "read"—on the level of image rather than narrative. Being used to analyzing complex word structures, I felt relieved. I didn't have to lecture; all I had to do was sit back and watch.

"Pather" is a Bengali word for path or road. "Panchali" refers to a series of songs or poems that make up the vernacular versions of the two great epics of Indian literature. While alluding to these epic tales, the novel by Bibhutibhushan Banerji on which Satyajit Ray's film is based deals with ordinary people. In 1969, I saw only *Pather Panchali,* the first of the films of Ray's trilogy, which continues with *Aparajito* and ends with *The World of Apu.*

The story begins with Apu's sister Durga, a lively and mischievous girl, who roams freely through the orchards of her neighbors, stealing fruit, which she shares with an aged "Auntie" who lives with her impoverished family. Durga's father Horihar, a well-educated man and would-be poet, barely makes a living performing religious rituals for local patrons. Durga's mother Shorbojoya, who struggles to make ends meet on her husband's meager income, expresses irritation with Auntie for depleting the family's food supply and with Durga for her wildness. To make matters worse, Auntie is complicit with Durga's petty thievery, not only because she benefits from it, but also because she takes pleasure in the girl's high-spirited company.

Into this family the treasured boy-child, Apu, is born. Shorbojoya, who can do nothing but find fault with her daughter, dotes on her son, preparing him special meals and fussing over his arrangements for school. Far from being envious of her brother or his privileged position in the family, Durga treats him with favor, sharing her precious booty of stolen fruit with him, shepherding him to school, and including him in her private games and adventures. Only once does she show obvious displeasure—when Apu takes bits of shiny paper from her box of playthings in order to make a toy crown for himself.

Durga behaves in a loving, even maternal, way toward her brother. Yet, when one of her adolescent girlfriends begins excitedly to prepare for marriage, Durga states that such a fate is not for her. As time passes and the family's fortunes continue to decline, Horihar decides to go on the road looking for work. In his absence, Shorbojoya becomes more intolerant of Auntie and even more short tempered toward her daughter. Forced to leave the shelter of Shorbojoya's home, Auntie dies, exhausted, on the path through a bamboo thicket. Not long afterward, Durga and Apu, who have wandered in search of the far-distant railroad tracks, are caught in a heavy downpour. Reveling in the rain and wind, Durga stands in an open field, shaking her hair free and swinging it in a loose arc around her, while her brother crouches under a tree shivering. Durga, always somewhat in fragile health, falls ill with a fever, which nothing can relieve, including the nutritious food donated by a neighbor and her mother's sudden, but real, concern and tender care.

Until this point in the story, I did not see myself reflected in any of its characters, yet something about Durga's illness and the nature of her relationship with her mother began to feel familiar, touching on aspects of my own buried history.

Durga—so beautiful, animated, and graceful—dies. As if to signal such a violent narrative disruption, the film changes pace with the arrival of the monsoon. For a while, nothing happens in the human realm, as the camera lingers lovingly on images of the pond rippled by the wind, skimmed by water bugs, and dappled by the first drops of rain. These (almost still) shots have the clarity and simplicity of Japanese prints. Not only do they mark the change of seasons, but they also prepare for the lyric scene in the meadow where

Durga turns her face up to the rain, then bends and swings her long hair in the wind, as if performing a private dance of pleasure. This entire sequence is wordless, until the moment at which she joins her brother under the banyan tree and, wrapping her sari around him, begins to chant, "Rain, rain, go away."

Like the scene in the field, the drama of Durga's death unfolds without dialogue. Shorbojoya, aware of the gravity of her daughter's condition, attends her while she sleeps, moistening a cloth and placing it on her forehead to bring down her fever. Occasionally, Shorbojoya herself dozes off. Then a thunderstorm arises, signaling its arrival by a curtain blowing in the window, a shutter flapping, the door latch rattling and the flicker of a candle flame. Each of these disturbances increases in intensity until even the household deity threatens to fall from its shelf. Shorbojoya, anxious and fearful, continues to tend to the sleeping Durga as the storm worsens, finally causing the curtain to pull free and the door to break open. As Shorbojoya leaves her daughter's side to reattach the curtain and shut the door, Durga wakes, calling to her mother and reaching out her arms. Shorbojoya clasps her daughter to her, while lightning flashes into the room and the elephant deity sways dangerously. The next thing we hear is the insistent sound of a door knocker. It is morning, and Shorbojoya has sent Apu (who has slept through the storm) to fetch a neighbor.

As dramatic and affecting as this scene is, it did not make me cry. Instead, my reactions mirrored those of the bereaved Shorbojoya, who does not speak or give way to her grief until the return of her unsuspecting husband Horihar. In the immediate aftermath of her daughter's death, she sits cradling Durga's head in her lap, staring blankly into the middle distance. Some time later, as Apu prepares for school, brushing his teeth, combing his hair, and gathering his books and slate, she sits on the porch, her hair in disarray, with the same look of mute inconsolability.

If Shorbojoya's ravaged face seemed familiar to me, it was no doubt because it reflected that of my mother, who did not give voice to her own grief in the wake of my father's death. This was a face I had learned to live with, and as young as I was, my features had begun to assume the same expression.

I don't remember ever seeing my mother cry after my dad died. Maybe she did, and I have erased this memory. More likely, I believe, she concealed her grief, thinking that she was doing what was best. Such a stance would have fit with her own upbringing, and nothing in our middle-of-America life in the early 1950s pointed toward anything different. There were no bereavement self-help books then, no grief support groups, no friendly neighborhood therapists. Only people who were truly wacko went to see a psychiatrist. How was my mother to know that outright crying might have helped? She staked her future, instead, on dignity and self-restraint. Years later, when I watched Jackie Kennedy attending her children at her husband's gravesite, I thought of my mother. At thirty-four, my mother was a beautiful, young widow, determined to show the world a good face.

I took my mother's model for myself, doing what I could to suppress public signs of distress. This meant pretending that nothing had changed, that nothing had been lost. The ghost among us could never be named. Nor could his absence be mourned.

I did my best throughout my childhood to keep our family pact, as if our pain could be wished away by refusing to give in to it. Such a strategy may seem cold, yet the alternative may have felt worse. What if grief is a bottomless pit? What if you just shatter or disintegrate? Suppose you can't find a reason to get up in the morning, to comb your hair, or brush your teeth? What if you sink into a melancholy so deep that you can't go on?

Shorbojoya, sitting motionless and impassive on her porch, looked to me as if she were having such thoughts. But my family had got it all backward. Shorbojoya's lack of expressiveness locks her into her despair. When, at last, she gives way to her tears, it is a relief.

This moment occurs after Horihar returns to his severely damaged home, bringing gifts for every member of his family. As he begins happily recounting his successes, Shorbojoya moves silently into the house, returning with his smoking utensils, her face carefully shrouded in the folds of her sari. Standing with her back to him, she takes the picture of the goddess Lakshmi that he has brought her. It is when he hands her a new sari for Durga that she breaks down, no longer able to contain her sorrow. As Shorbojoya collapses in front of him, her cries of anguish represented by the keening notes of a *tarshehnai* played by Ravi Shankar, Horihar awakens to the reality of his loss. He falls across his wife's crumpled body, equally devastated, weeping with her.

In Shorbojoya's contorted face and the exquisite pitch of Ravi Shankar's music, I encountered an image and an echo of something within me. My body heard this call and responded in the only way it knew how—viscerally. I felt a ripple in my mid-section, which rose up through my chest and esophagus in a powerful contraction. I was not used to crying like this. I was not used to crying at all—it was as if I inhabited an emotional landscape so parched that I had no interior water table from which to draw. In the small Sahara of my heart, I had forgotten how to weep. Instead, I was convulsed, choking, snorting, and sobbing. My body claimed me in that moment, as surely as it had when I was ill as a child with rheumatic fever, asserting its rights, its private (and to me indecipherable) voice of pain.

Once I had begun to cry, I couldn't stop. My body was in a state of spasm, as determined to expel its store of bitter tears as it had been to empty the contents of my stomach in the early months of my pregnancy. I clutched Frank's arm, trying to hide my face against his chest. I knew that I was making a spectacle of myself. As soon as the credits appeared on the screen, I lurched out of my seat and stumbled toward the nearest exit. Once home, I continued to cry—deep, wrenching sobs, cast up from somewhere in my belly, like blood clots.

My husband, though sympathetic, was as bewildered as I was. He held me, rocked me, fetched me Kleenex, until I began to relax. I don't remember trying to discuss what had happened. As a result, I don't know what went through his head that night, whether he considered me unstable, perhaps even hysterical, or merely unpredictable. I think we were both grateful, once the tidal wave of emotion had passed, to fall, exhausted, into bed.

Frank had his own difficulties. His depression was something I was familiar with. It stopped him from writing papers in graduate school and nearly immobilized him when he felt most helpless about his relation to the Vietnam War and the draft. But he had discovered a passion for photography and pursued his goal of becoming a visual artist with conviction and energy. The days he spent alone in the house reading science-fiction novels did not disturb me. Most of our friends, after all, shared his anomie, for which we found more than enough cause in the country's political struggles and upheavals. What with my job teaching, being pregnant, and trying to finish my dissertation, I did not feel that I had the luxury to be depressed, which I associated with losing heart and doing nothing. Like my mother in the aftermath of my father's death, I was used to bearing up. I would do my duty, no matter how I felt. I would endure, no matter what.

Not suspecting the extent to which I shared my husband's depression (though mine took a different, more stoic form), I could not begin to fathom the reason for my breakdown in the face of a shadowy screen image. I was surprised and embarrassed, but, above all, at a loss. I set it aside as an anomaly. I did not want to talk about it, hoping that none of my friends or colleagues had witnessed my collapse.

A door had opened, allowing me a glimpse of something, and then had slammed shut. I was as ignorant of the contents of my mind and heart as I was of my swollen abdomen, which, taut and opaque, concealed its ripening burden for another three months. I was headed for a new destination, with no idea of how I was going to arrive. The only thing I understood with certainty is that I no longer had a choice. Something inside me was bound to come out.

At some point early in my pregnancy I stopped reading my childbirth books, because they were filled with stories of things that could go wrong. I found that I couldn't tolerate the explicit kinds of anxiety they induced in me, much less the nightmares I began to have of giving birth to something incomplete or deformed. Having difficulty imagining myself as a mother, I took obscure consolation in the predictions I received (based on my baby's heartbeat and my carriage) that I would have a boy. A father, I believed, would know how to raise a son, thus letting me off the hook.

In 1969, there was no such thing as ultrasound. In Vermont at that time, there weren't even any natural childbirth classes that my university-affiliated obstetrician knew of to recommend. When I asked about his use of anesthesia, he told me not to worry. "It'll be there if you need it," he said. This was the extent of our conversation about labor and delivery. Still, given my history of rheumatic fever, including some warnings that giving birth might be hard on my heart, I felt relieved to be associated with a research and teaching hospital. I tried not to think about how I was going to accomplish the task of moving my baby out of the burrow in my body she so tenaciously inhabited and hoped for the best. I was used to procrastinating about things that frightened or worried me, though I knew that pregnancy was different. You could ignore it for a while, perhaps, but it wasn't something you could just forget.

I was about two weeks past my due date when I started having contractions. The day before, I had had a sudden burst of energy and spent the entire morning raking dead leaves away from the flower beds in our backyard. Although it was late April, there was a chill in the air, and the daffodil shoots were just beginning to poke through their soggy mulch. Was my body, ordinarily so bulky and difficult to maneuver, aware of its impending change of state? Or did my unaccustomed exercise remind my sluggish womb of its most urgent task? Near dawn the next morning, I woke with definite muscular contractions, which I timed at five minutes apart.

The early stages of labor unfolded with textbook smoothness. I was uncomfortable, but not to the extent of being incapacitated. I woke my husband, ate breakfast, washed and dried my hair, and gathered my things for the hospital, a thirty-minute drive from where we lived. By noon when we arrived, my contractions inexplicably stopped, which embarrassed me and made me feel apologetic. Maybe I had succumbed to a false alarm! Yet I was admitted to a private room, handed a hospital gown, examined, shaved, and given an enema. At this point, the pains, much to my relief, began to recur. I had not misinterpreted the signals from my mountainous mid-section. This was the real thing.

Nothing I had read or heard about, however, prepared me for what followed. Although my doctor had told me on my last visit that I was going to have a large baby, I had no idea what that might mean, least of all any notion of how her big head was going to emerge from the pursed mouth of my womb or the tender opening of my vagina. Perhaps this is just as well. Had I tried to visualize this process, I might have been seized with panic.

The hospital staff was not only unequipped for natural childbirth, they also believed in banishing fathers from the labor and delivery rooms. I was told to bid farewell to my husband at precisely the moment when I needed him most. For the better part of my labor, I was left alone, with only occasional visits from nurses and doctors, none of whom showed sympathy for my ordeal. Once, when I gave up on being stoic and groaned aloud—as women in other rooms were doing—I heard a doctor in the hallway comment, "Tell her to stop that, she's just wasting her energy."

For reasons I still don't understand, I did not experience relief in between contractions. Rather, I felt in the grip of continuous pain. At one point, when my doctor offered to administer a paracervical block and asked whether I was having a contraction, I didn't reply, since I couldn't tell the difference. "Surely you know," he barked impatiently, as if I were deliberately withholding this vital piece of information—or were just plain stupid.

A resident injected the cervical anesthetic, which either didn't do any good or held my pain at its current (nearly intolerable) level. Much later, I was given a shot of Demerol, which did seem to help. Around this time, the contractions began to behave the way the books said they should, and I found that I could rest in the oasis-like intervals between them. At last, they told me I could push. But just as I began to feel the satisfaction of cooperating with my body's effort, instead of merely enduring it, I was told to stop. Things were going too quickly, and the delivery room wasn't ready.

By the time I was moved to a stretcher and wheeled in for delivery, I was so exhausted that I didn't even consider protesting the spinal anesthetic they had prepared. "Good," I thought, "at least this part won't hurt." I lay back, barely able to see over the mound of my belly, listening to the doctors coolly discussing my progress. They performed an episiotomy (again without asking) and laid bets on my baby's birth weight. I remember seeing a bright spurt of blood on the obstetrician's white jacket and thinking that it looked beautiful, like the enormous red poppies painted by Georgia O'Keeffe. When I lifted my head in order to get a better view of the momentous event taking place at the lower end of my body, someone reprimanded me. "Put your head down," this voice snapped, as if I were a naughty child deliberately disobeying orders. Only later did I learn that with a spinal it's important to lie flat. Otherwise you may wind up with a splitting headache.

"He's going to be a little football player," I heard next, as my round, fully formed baby began to emerge. Then, "Oh, it's a girl," as she slid out completely. In this stunned moment, I made a connection that had eluded me throughout my pregnancy and labor. At the end of it all, there is a gift. My body's nine-month metamorphosis and journey through a pain so intense that it had seemed a timeless world of its own had produced this astonishing result. With no conscious will or intent, I had made a living, breathing human being. What's more, I had made her beautiful, I had made her perfect.

Birthing my daughter Jessica was the hardest work I had ever done. It was also completely involuntary, not unlike the way I had cried at *Pather Panchali*. Somehow these two events seemed connected, but I couldn't see how. All I knew in the spring of 1969 is that I had made contact with myself in a way that was electrifying, not through my intellect, which ceaselessly invented words for my convoluted thought processes, but through my body and my emotions. Both seemed messy and somewhat alien.

Because my pain was so all encompassing, I could not escape it to some other, mental space in my head. It fused me (for the first time in my adult life) with my flesh. Never had I understood so completely how we shared the same fate. My body, I fleetingly comprehended, was not the carrier of my immaterial self, but its very ground and reality.

I wonder sometimes how I could have been so ignorant. Also why it was pain, rather than pleasure, that woke me up. How I wish I could say that it was my body's capacity for enjoyment that brought me back to myself. It would make a much better story. But the truth is that only something as relentless as physical pain could get my attention. Only pain, in its utter supremacy, could make the point.

At a certain pitch and intensity, pain is such a pure state of being that it annihilates normal categories of selfhood. Your mind's ceaseless chatter evaporates. You stop thinking in words. You cannot imagine a past or a future; you are bound to the present as to a wheel of fire. There are no adequate metaphors for this experience. Like visionary states of awareness, the condition of being in pain slips through the net of language. Unlike the mystic's spiritual transport, however, pain knocks you off your horse and throws you to the ground. If you are converted to anything by pain it is to the will and might of the body, to the weight of material existence.

My experience of giving birth was a revelation of this order. My body, I discovered, had an expressive language of its own, an inner volition and capacity for invention that I hadn't previously divined. It had also lost its smooth impermeability. A breach had occurred, which opened a channel from the innermost recess of my being to the world outside. I felt like Pandora, cracking the lid of her box. What other secrets, wishes, and possibilities lay hidden within?

It's no surprise to me now that I cried as I did at *Pather Panchali*. The enormous, though fragile, vessel of myself was about to break, spilling everything I had fought to keep inside. Years later, in the middle of a particularly soothing massage, I found myself thinking "I have made my body a container for my grief." Resentful of such an impossible task, my body had begun to fight back.

Once, when I was nursing Jessica, I had the almost hallucinatory sensation of being three women at once—my mother, my daughter, and myself. I was feeling the continuity of life (like the flow of milk through my breasts) circulate between and among us. Witnessing the mother/daughter drama in *Pather Panchali* stirred a different, but equally powerful current. I found myself as much in the high-spirited and unconventional girl who does not live to grow up as in the mother so devastated by her loss that she feels drained of her own interest in life. I was both daughter and mother myself, my pregnancy the sign of this crossroads condition. In January of 1969, I could not give voice to these emotions, much less recognize them as separate feeling states. Yet, judging from the magnitude of my physical reaction, I would say that Ray's film touched the nerve center of my own history— my childhood grief at my father's death and my response to my mother's suppressed mourning, both of which fed my anxiety about my impending maternity.

Like Durga, I had been gravely ill as an adolescent, suffering from my last and most debilitating attack of rheumatic fever at age eleven. I would guess that my immune system, already vulnerable to strep infection, was further weakened by the sadness that engulfed my family in the wake of my father's death. My pediatrician had warned my mother to expect a relapse. As frightened and grief-stricken as me, she could not have known how to prevent such an occurrence. Maybe she even considered it inevitable, yet another instance of our family's bad luck. When, in time, I did fall ill, she quit her new job as an office receptionist and devoted herself to nursing me.

For weeks, perhaps longer, I did not get better, despite my high-protein diet and regimen of total bed rest. I was sore and aching all over, with inflammation in all of my joints. Nothing seemed to alleviate this pain, which was taking its most insidious toll deep within my chest. No illness could have been more symbolically appropriate. My affliction had invaded my cardiac valves. I was sick at heart.

My mother decided to ask a family friend, who had suffered from rheumatic fever himself as a child, to take a look at me. Although this man was a doctor, he was not a specialist in children's heart disease, like the one who had been treating me for years. After spending an hour or so talking to me and my mother and listening to my heart, he made a simple recommendation. "Why not try penicillin?" My own doctor, who had been treating me conservatively (perhaps not wanting to prescribe a relatively new and untested drug), agreed. Slowly, I began to make progress.

What stands out for me now about this moment is not that I began to receive a new form of treatment but that my mother seemed frightened as she talked about me to the visiting doctor. Perhaps because he was a friend, she let more of her feelings show. I sensed her uncertainty about my future. Despite the best medical treatment and her near-constant care, I was not improving. Rather, I was slipping away from her.

It had not occurred to me until this point that my illness might be irreversible. A new thought took shape in my mind—I might die. When I had been ill before, I had gotten well. Even though I was much sicker this time, I trusted my mother to pull me through. Suddenly, I became aware that she herself was not confident about this outcome. A terrifying prospect opened; we were equally helpless.

I wanted my mother to save me, perhaps as she had pulled my older brother to safety while my father was drowning. Although she had rescued my brother, she hadn't been able to save my dad, who was already out of reach. Was he swept away? Was I, too, beyond her grasp? Maybe love wasn't enough. I began to be afraid for myself.

The wordless drama of Durga's death was one I silently understood. I felt the love and longing between mother and daughter, as well as their fear and impotence. Some part of me felt like Durga, who succumbs to her illness. Would I also be like Shorbojoya, unable to protect or save a life?

While Durga's death touched on my fears about my own survival in the aftermath of my father's death, I did not break down crying until Shorbojoya releases her pent-up tears. At this point, I responded so overwhelmingly that I let go of my inhuman efforts at self-control. Crying this way may have shamed me in public, but it released a deeper need to acknowledge my long-withheld terror and sadness.

Shorbojoya's breakdown communicates the news of Durga's death to Horihar, whose face first registers confusion, then horrified realization. My outburst of tears, so far removed from their point of origin, made far less sense. Neither I nor my husband understood why I was upset. It was, after all, only a movie.

I was so unused to knowing what I felt that I could hardly begin to fathom the realignment taking place in me that frigid January night. It was as if some sub-oceanic tectonic plate had begun to buckle and heave, altering my interior landscape.

After years of quiescence, my body was waking up. It had an urgent message, but no words as such with which to communicate. It was like an infant, using everything at its command to get a primary message across. "Come here," it was saying, or "Feed me," or "I don't want to be alone." But I wasn't used to honoring my emotional needs. How, I wondered, could I possibly take care of another, vulnerable human being? How could I become a mother?

Pather Panchali confronted me with an excruciating paradox. Where I loved most deeply, I also felt the most potential for failure and loss. I didn't know how to view my voluminous pregnancy—as the manifestation of my body's creativity or the sign of its essential emptiness. Was I hollow or full? Capable or helpless? These were not questions I was used to asking myself.

I knew nothing about child rearing. I barely knew how to keep house and cook. Somehow I had bypassed the domestic arts in the process of growing up. I had never bathed a baby or even changed a diaper, much less watched a mother breastfeed her infant. Luckily, Jessica was not difficult. She took to my nipple with an ease and naturalness that astounded me. She was a "good little nurser," as my hospital attendant said. Being so fully formed at birth, she was also a sound sleeper, but I knew there was more to mothering than that.

My daughter was so beautiful I was almost afraid of touching her. As if I might alter her perfection somehow. I didn't feel worthy of her, as if I might contaminate or infect her. As if the place she had come from was too damaged to provide nurturance. At the same time, I felt a gratitude and passion for her existence that bound me to the destiny wrapped up in her, like some kind of hidden treasure or secret. More than anything, I wanted to become a mother who could hold her hand, pointing her down the road she herself could walk.

Pather Panchali includes, over its course, a birth, a marriage, two deaths, and an exodus. The film ends with an image of the abandoned family home, open now to the encroachments of the surrounding forest, and the road that leads Apu and his parents away from their village to the city of Benares. From a long shot, we view the ruined house and garden, as a snake slithers slowly across the porch toward the interior of the empty dwelling. Father, mother, and child, meanwhile, sit huddled together in their ox-drawn, covered wagon, with a single swaying lantern to light their path.

By the fall of 1971, my husband, daughter, and I were preparing to leave Middlebury. After a long delay, Frank had received a 1-Y draft deferment, perhaps finally on the basis of his paternity. My teaching contract had not been renewed, however, and we were forced to find other employment. After months of fruitless search, I was offered a job at a Midwestern university in a metropolitan center large enough for Frank to find work. I had finished my Ph.D. at last and felt poised to begin a new life. We were leaving behind a dream of simple rural existence that we had both shared on moving to Vermont. We had thought of this little valley cradled between the Green and Adirondack mountains as an ideal place to make a home. The reality of small-town college life— ingrown, gossipy, and often cruel to newcomers—had been a shock to us both. With our unconventional family structure of artist father and working mother, we just didn't fit. It seemed like a good idea, at this point, to choose a more cosmopolitan environment. Another road was calling us, though neither of us could anticipate what lay ahead.

Silences:

House of Cards

> Children suffer not (I think) less than their elders,
> but differently.
>
> ⟋ C. S. Lewis, *Surprised by Joy*

I WAS IN MY FIFTIES before I asked my younger brother Ron, who was seven years old when our father drowned, whether he remembered anyone comforting him in the days and weeks immediately following Dad's death. His answer shocked me. "I was too young," he said, "to deserve such deference."

I'm not sure what prompted me to ask. I think I wanted someone to confirm my own memory of isolation in the aftermath of my dad's disappearance. My brother's statement made me feel ashamed. Whereas I felt aggrieved, even angry, about the lack of attention to my distress as a child, Ron didn't seem to mind. It didn't occur to him that, being so young, he was especially needy or vulnerable. I wondered if he was used to being overlooked. While my older brother Bob and I actively vied for our parents' favor, Ron seemed more content to sit on the sidelines, a quiet observer. Perhaps he didn't feel that his position had radically changed.

For me, my dad's absence was like a sudden eclipse. What had been warm was now cold; light was now dark. My mother, preoccupied with her own grief, was too far away from me to help. Like my brother Ron, I began to efface myself, allowing the chatter of my wishes, needs, and desires to subside—slowly falling silent.

Shy by nature already, I became even more subdued. My voice became softer, my thoughts more private and increasingly difficult to articulate. Gradually, I lost confidence in my ability to be heard, much less to say what I meant. Over time, my silence seemed to matter less. Being quiet had its advantages. You couldn't be punished for something you felt but didn't say. Also, if you never expressed a definite opinion no one could gauge the extent of your ignorance. Like Ron, I became an observer, watchful for cues on how to behave, so as to draw the least amount of attention to myself. Otherwise, I found solace in reading, which provided an alternative universe where happy endings were the norm. I preferred a world of make-believe to the drab reality of my loss.

Something like this happens in Michael Lessac's film *House of Cards* to six-year-old Sally when her architect father dies on an expedition to shore up Mayan ruins. She is so precocious and seemingly unperturbed by this tragic disruption in her life, that no one notices how she is struggling to make sense of a world suddenly gone crazy, how desperate she is for someone to provide meaning in her fractured universe. In this frame of mind, she turns to her Indian guide, who offers a mythological explanation of life and death that Sally takes to heart and later acts on.

The film opens with a voice-over dialogue between Sally and her Indian guide.

"Why do people dream?" Sally asks.

"To see things better," her guide replies.

The gods, he says, live "in every living thing." They made people because they were bored and wanted entertainment. The grandmother of light gave humans the power to see inside one another, but they abused their power, and today it is given only to special children in the form of dreams, where there are no words.

"Why are there no words?" Sally asks.

"Because it is easier to see without words," the guide explains. "The special children see the world as it really wants to be."

Sally is asking serious questions about the nature of her dramatically altered life. The answers she receives are symbolic, not meant to be taken in the word-for-word way she absorbs them. "People don't die," her guide says, "they go from one home to another." Later, when he says that her father "lives always," Sally interrogates him closely.

"Where does Daddy live now?"

"In the cradle moon."

"But how can he get there? How can he possibly get there when he's dead?"

"Shh. Remember. Sometimes you have to be very quiet to see things."

Sally, who was three when her family left for Central America and cannot remember any other home, goes to sleep with this comforting thought. Her father lives, she thinks, in the crescent moon, and if she is "quiet" enough, she can see him—perhaps even find a way to visit him there.

I believe there is a time early in life when fantasy and reality are inseparable. Only gradually do we learn to distinguish between dream and waking, between the world of fact and that of imagination. Art can be especially vivid during this time, entering us on the primary level of the senses—virtually without obstruction. As children, we may be the greatest consumers of art; we mainline it.

My daughter Jessica was somewhere around three when her dad and I took her to see her first play, a Children's Theatre Company performance of *Peter and the Wolf*. Although we sat well back from the stage, Jessica was made very anxious by the presence of the adult-size wolf.

"Will the wolf eat me?" she kept asking.

"No," I said, "it's not a real wolf. He's just pretending. It's like a story."

But Jessica's fears were not assuaged. This was no picture-book wolf. He was full of life and only a stone's throw away. She continued to worry until she came up with a solution of her own.

"I know why the wolf won't eat me," she announced, at last. "Because I'm too big!"

Jess hadn't really grasped the distinction I was trying to make. In her mind, the wolf was still alive and threatening. She was simply too large for him to swallow. It was a matter of years before she understood clearly the nature of theatrical illusion. I remember the moment when this slippery concept took hold.

Jess was six or seven years old, a veteran by now of the Children's Theatre Company. She especially enjoyed the post-performance ritual of shaking hands with the players (still in costume) in the theater vestibule. This time, we had gone to see *Raggedy Ann and Andy,* with young adolescent actors playing the soft, floppy dolls. After going through the line once to shake hands, Jess wanted to do it again. Not wishing to break the spell of her enchantment, I said yes. The second time, she circled slowly around the dolls, inspecting them from the back. When she was finished, she returned to me and her dad.

"They're not real dolls," she pronounced, with finality. "They just have suits on!"

If the world of make-believe frightened my daughter in the form of a wolf who might eat her, the same world soothes Sally in *House of Cards* into thinking that her deceased father lives in the moon. When her family returns to their Southern farmhouse home, she falls eerily silent, concentrating inwardly on her vision of this possibility. Sally's mother Ruth is so absorbed in the process of settling back into her former life that she fails to notice her daughter's distraction. Only Sally's brother Michael, who is old enough to have a realistic understanding of death, is aware that something is wrong. When Michael's toy airplane crashes into the chimney of the house, Sally, who associates high places with her father's new home, calmly ascends the steeply pitched roof to retrieve it. Later, on her first day at school, she spies a tree that seems made for climbing and begins to ascend. When a classmate follows her lead and then falls, breaking his arm, the school authorities become alarmed. Sally's refusal to talk triggers further inquiry, and a psychologist is sent to her home to investigate. By the time he arrives, Sally has embarked on another daredevil adventure, climbing out onto the roof, at Michael's request, to recover a baseball that has become lodged in the gutter.

What no one but Michael knows is that Sally, who is fearless about height, goes into a panic in the face of any sudden change in her environment. When Ruth, attempting to rescue her daughter from what she perceives as imminent danger, climbs out onto the roof and (in an unconscious gesture) turns her baseball cap around on her head, Sally freezes in her tracks, uttering a series of sharp, staccato cries. Only when Ruth, prompted by the psychologist, reverses her cap does Sally recover herself, retracing her steps along the gutter with the ease of a practiced aerialist.

Sally's suddenly altered behavior resembles that of the autistic children in the psychologist's clinic, but Ruth resists such a diagnosis. She does not want Sally treated as abnormal, yet she cannot ignore the fact that something is awry. Sally seems to have withdrawn into a completely private reality, refusing to speak or utter a sound other than the distress signal she emits when the immediate order of her universe is disturbed. And she continues to climb, fascinated by any structure that offers closer proximity to the tantalizing curve of the sickle moon. Finally, when Sally ventures out onto a crane at an unfinished construction site, Ruth has to face the self-destructive potential in her daughter's fascination with height.

It isn't that Sally wants to die. She just wants to be closer to her dad, who seems both impossibly remote and tantalizingly within reach. Dreamily, she contemplates the moon from her perch on her bedroom windowsill, listening to a whispered interior monologue that has more reality than any of the actual conversations swirling around her. Sally is obeying the instructions of her Indian guide—to the letter. Only in this way can she sustain the illusion that nothing has been lost.

Unlike Sally, I didn't stop speaking when my dad died, nor did I engage in high-risk behavior. For a girl in the 1950s, I didn't seem all that abnormal. But I did stop saying what I thought and felt. Over time, there were fewer and fewer things I could talk about. Silence became a habit, assuming a will of its own. I didn't control it; it controlled me.

For years, the only place where I was comfortable speaking my mind was in the highly structured and predictable environment of school, and even then I preferred to listen to my teachers lecture, taking meticulous notes in my neat, backhand script. When I did raise my hand, my face would flush, and my heart would pound in anticipation of praise or disapproval. More than anything, I wanted my teachers to like me. I studied hard, in quest of the "right" answers. Being smart in my mind translated into being good—even being loved.

Quietness and obedience go a long way toward success in school. In this, I had the distinct advantage over my unruly, and equally intelligent, older brother, whose restlessness in the classroom won him frequent knuckle raps with a ruler. One teacher, no doubt at the end of her rope, told him point-blank that he was an idiot. I was too young, and too competitive, to register his distress. From the beginning, I had played "second" to his lordly first. If anything, I probably took satisfaction in the edge I had finally gained in our heated sibling rivalry. I was determined to wrest my father's posthumous love from him by doing the one thing I felt confident about. If nothing else, I knew I could get A's on my report card.

By the time I got to college, I was more than shy; I was distant and intimidating. I had no language for the life of my emotions other than that provided by my obsessive fiction-reading—much of which was suffused with a hothouse atmosphere of Victorian restraint. I was a great reader of nineteenth-century novels, but their byzantine social conventions and equally convoluted sentences did nothing to prepare me for the reality of coming of age in the *American Graffiti* world of the early 1960s. I could easily imagine myself in the place of passionate Jane Eyre, beautiful Natasha Rostov, or intellectual Dorothea Brooke. Yet I hadn't the faintest idea of how to talk to a boy I liked or what to do on a first date. I was not only tongue-tied and awkward, I was completely out of step with my generation. I was also fixated, in a way that I could only understand as weird or morbid, on death.

My outlook on life was serious and tragic. Having a father who died young had marked me, I felt. I was convinced that I had seen some dark truth that my boy and clothes-crazy peers had not. It was this harrowing awareness that made me different, that singled me out. Being melancholic, however, does not make you popular. On the contrary, it scares people off. Those who do not shy away tend to reflect your own darkness back.

In college, I met a woman whose reticence, inner pre-occupation, and passion for academic excellence not only matched but exceeded mine. She was intellectual, self-disciplined, and emotionally intense. She was also suicidal. My friendship with her introduced a small, but significant, voice of doubt about the course of social isolation I had set for myself.

I met Anne my freshman year at Bryn Mawr, a small women's college proud of its feminist heritage and celebrated for the independence of its graduates. Anne's room was one of the coveted "singles," just across the hall from mine, a double I shared with a mostly incompatible roommate. Anne, in contrast, was a kindred soul. She was someone whose nature I recognized. She was cool, composed, highly self-motivated, and ambitious. I was more than a little afraid of her.

Slowly we entered into conversation, mostly in the hallways as we passed each other to and from meals or on the way to the communal bathroom. We shared stories about how many hours we studied, how little sleep we got. We were equally obsessed with work. The harder our courses—the more books we read or papers we had to write—the more significance we attached to our grades. We seemed to be competing with each other—but for what? For some ill-defined goal of who could suffer the most in the pursuit of academic distinction? I didn't understand my attraction to Anne, but sensed that she was someone with as complex a personal history as my own. She was someone I could talk to.

There is a moment in *House of Cards,* at the clinic for autistic children where Sally's condition is being evaluated, when her mother comes across two young people who are contentedly conversing by reciting prime numbers to each other. Ruth, who grasps the means of their communication, manages to join in this eerie interchange by bringing a book of prime numbers from which she makes her own contributions. The children recognize her "speech" and make a place for her in their private circle.

Neither Anne nor I was autistic, but we recognized something in each other. Long before we began to talk, we understood that in some fundamental way we were alike. While neither of us had any insight into our personal history, we recognized each other's intellectual aspirations. This was our starting point.

One Saturday night, when most of the dorm was vacated, we took a coffee break from our studies in Anne's room. We began by commenting on our professors—expressing frustration at their expectations, admiration for the ones we wished to emulate and contempt for those we did not.

Slowly our conversation drifted to a more personal plane, as we began to exchange stories about growing up. Anne had been adopted by a woman whose first husband had died young. Although Anne appreciated her adoptive mother's kindness and goodwill, she hated the man her mother had subsequently married, whom she referred to as her "stepfather." She bore a deep grudge against him for sending her to a public high school and for thinking that the state university was a good enough place for her to finish her education. With her mother's help, she had fought and won the battle to attend Bryn Mawr, the college of her choice. Anne also revealed to me her plan—to comprehend all of Western civilization and to graduate at the top of her class.

I had always thought of myself as smart and ambitious, but in Anne I felt I had met my match. In the naïve way of a nineteen-year-old, I wanted to absorb everything there was to learn, but I also wanted to marry and have children. My intellectual precocity served an obscure, but deeper, aim. I wanted to make my father proud of me by following in his footsteps. It wasn't so much abstract knowledge I craved, as approval.

Anne's temperament was more severe than mine. After sharing with her the story of my father's death and confessing my active dislike for my own stepfather, I was startled by her point-blank question: "Have you ever considered suicide?" While I knew that my stepfather had had suicidal tendencies and had at least once taken an overdose, I was in the habit of avoiding this awareness, not wanting to consider the nature of his unhappiness, which might open a door in myself that I needed to keep closed. "No," I said quickly, instantly recalling the teaching of the Catholic Church, most of whose prohibitions I had long since decided to ignore.

Suicide, I had learned in my grade-school catechism, was an act of despair. Its irreversibility makes it the one sin that God will not forgive. The logic behind this thinking is elegantly simple. Once you are dead, you have no opportunity to repent. For this reason, God, as even the tortured Hamlet knows, "has fixed his canon 'gainst self-slaughter." As confused as I was about the place of my childhood religion in my life, I found this doctrine oddly reassuring. It prevented me from thinking about how bad you would have to feel in order to want to die.

The moment when death bursts into a child's consciousness is shocking. Before this, death may be a word in one's vocabulary, but it has no concrete reality. Once, when my brother Ron was very young, he asked my mother if he could have my grandmother's bedside radio when she died. I don't think he was being callous. More likely, he was fascinated by this new and exciting object and wanted one for himself. Attaching no real meaning to death, he was not embarrassed to express his desire. I didn't understand death any better than

Ron until our father died. Even then, I didn't want to believe in its finality.

I remember the moment when my daughter began to take in the reality of death. One day, in the early spring, when the snow packs had shrunk enough to expose patches of bare earth, my neighbor Eric invited me and Jessica on a nature walk with his family in a wildflower garden not far from where we lived. I bundled four-year-old Jess into her snow-suit, boots, mittens, and scarf, and we set out with our friends, who took pleasure in naming the variety of return-ing birds, the newly budding plants and trees. Suddenly Eric, who had a particularly keen eye, pointed to a mound of matted leaves and fur not far from the trail.

"Look kids," he exclaimed, "it's a squirrel."

One by one, each of his three children approached the de-composing mass and took turns poking it with a stick. Then, losing interest, they skipped after their mother, who had walked on ahead.

When our turn came to inspect what was left of the squir-rel, Jess stood looking at it, transfixed. She wanted to know what had happened and why. Trying to sound matter-of-fact, I explained that the squirrel had died.

"Why he die for?" she asked.

"Because it was time for him to die," I said. "Because everything dies sometime. It's a part of nature." I hoped I was sounding as confident as Eric.

"People die?"

This was precisely the question I was most afraid of. Un-like Sally's Indian guide, I had no spiritual, religious, or mythological wisdom to provide.

"Yes," I said, taking her hand and pulling her gently away from the squirrel.

Something about this experience struck home. Despite my best attempts to divert Jessica's attention from the dead squirrel, she kept begging to go back for another look. Squeamishly, I refused. I didn't know how to answer her repeated question, "Why he die for?" Nor did I particularly want to dwell on the squirrel's decaying remains. I hadn't resolved my own feelings about death and felt at a loss to explain such a mystery to my daughter.

Once this subject had taken hold in Jessica's imagination, it did not go away. She examined it from many angles over the course of that year, in much the same way that she had inspected the costumes of Raggedy Ann and Andy. She began to collect pieces of information about death, mulling them over until she had arrived at an explanation that made sense to her. With sometimes startling results.

Several days after a trip to the children's room of the Bell Museum of Natural History, where visitors are allowed to handle animal pelts and bones, she asked about what happens after death. I told her something about funerals and burial practices. She listened for a while and then interrupted.

"When people die," she observed, "they take the skin off but leave the faces on." For a stunned moment, I worried about what kind of fantasies she might be having. Then I realized that she was generalizing from animals to humans, based on what she had seen in the museum.

Death had begun to have texture, but it had yet to touch someone my daughter knew. It had no finality in human terms. Something that happened later in the summer alerted me to the nature of her confusion. One of her playmates wandered away from a birthday celebration held at a Minneapolis lake and nearly drowned. By the time he was found, he was facedown in the water. An ambulance was summoned, while someone administered mouth-to-mouth resuscitation. Fortunately, the child revived. When Jess came home, she was full of this story.

"When you die," she said with conviction, "they take you to the hospital. And the doctors bring you back to life."

In a backhand way, my daughter had learned about life after death—a concept that she applied to all and sundry. A teenage friend and sometime baby-sitter had taken her to see the movie *Jesus Christ Superstar,* which had made a big impression. "God dive," she would say solemnly—not quite getting the distinction between "die" and "dive." If Christ had died on the cross and then come back to life, why then anyone could. Her child's logic was impeccable—and nearly impossible to refute. It was giving me a headache to keep track of her misconceptions. It was also breaking my heart to tell her the truth.

We reached another turning point.

Not long after we had moved to Minnesota, the poet John Berryman committed suicide. He jumped to his death from a bridge that connects the east and west banks of the University of Minnesota campus. Although we lived in the same neighborhood, I never had a chance to meet him. Jessica, however, played with a group of neighborhood kids that included his youngest daughter, who was still a baby when her father died. I didn't think about this much until one day, some years later, when Jess, chattering away from the backseat of the car, offered her most serious pronouncement about death.

"Some people just don't want to live," she declared.

"That's true," I said, a little unnerved, but plunging ahead regardless. I was thinking about Berryman and wondering if Jessica had somehow heard this explanation of his death from one of her playmates—who, in turn, would have gotten it from an adult. On the whole, it seemed the kindest and most neutral way of describing a painful reality. I couldn't bring myself to lie about this.

"But most people *do* want to live, just the same," I hastened to reassure her.

Although in college my friend Anne talked about suicide as a philosophical issue, I sensed that she (as much as Berryman) was unsure about whether she wanted to live. Many years later, when I heard of her sudden, unaccounted-for death on a Friday the 13th, I felt certain that she had made her choice. It would be like her to depart on a note of wicked humor.

Neither Anne nor I had much insight into our family histories. We each had a list of losses and injuries that we could tick off at the drop of a hat, but no awareness of what to do about them. Surviving—and overachieving—was enough, we thought. Eventually, I suspect, even the very tangible rewards of overachievement paled for Anne before a deeper seduction—the siren call of surcease.

I was in my second year of graduate study when I heard about Anne's death. We had each, as it happens, graduated *summa,* among the top four students in our class. I won a Woodrow Wilson fellowship; she won a Fulbright. We were both double majors—she in German and Archeology, I in French and English. Year by year, we vied with each other over who took the most demanding course load, who studied more, or who deprived herself of the most sleep. We were neck and neck in our race for academic honors, even beyond graduation. Until the news of Anne's death, which brought me up short. Being so like her in my single-minded pursuit of academic excellence, I began to fear that I would come to the same end.

I had thought of my attraction to death as an intellectual passion, something like falling in love with a dead poet—or romanticizing the tragedies in other peoples' lives. No doubt Anne's history had appealed to me in this way. In her, I saw someone whose suffering, though different from mine, was equally intense. But likeness was not enough to sustain even a friendship. We were each so inwardly preoccupied that we couldn't help each other.

Anne was not only more ambitious than I, she was also more silent, more remote. There were days when we passed in the dorm hallway that I hesitated to speak to her. It seemed too much of an intrusion. I also feared, in some obscure way, that she looked down on me. In my own shyness, I may have conveyed the same impression. After Anne's death, I was more frightened than drawn to the emotional state she seemed to inhabit. From the outside, it looked like stone cold refusal.

It is Sally's remoteness, in *House of Cards,* that is scary and even life threatening. Combined with her inner absorption, her fascination with high places constitutes a kind of death wish, to which she alone is oblivious. Not fully grasping the finality of her father's departure, she does not understand that reunion with him in the moon can only occur at the expense of her own life.

The question the film poses is how such a child may be rescued from the world of hopeful illusion she inhabits without destroying either her creativity or her ability to live with the reality of her loss. This delicate task is given to Sally's mother, who, once she perceives just how far Sally has traveled away from her, does her utmost to woo her back. The turning point in this process occurs when Ruth realizes that, in order to communicate with her stubbornly silent daughter, she must find some way to enter her universe. "She's alone somewhere," Ruth tries to explain to the well-meaning but somewhat pedestrian psychologist. "She may not talk, but that doesn't mean she's not trying to tell me something." Ruth sets out to decipher her daughter's private language, as earlier she had tried to enter the tête-à-tête of the children who converse in prime numbers. She finds the clue she is seeking in Sally's elaborately and delicately constructed house of cards.

Gathering all the packs of playing cards she can find in her house, Sally builds an open spiral out of smaller triangles, with just enough space inside for her to sit. Recognizing the uniqueness of this creation, Ruth photographs it from all angles before the finely poised structure collapses. Later, she uses her architect's skill to simulate it on her computer. Then, in an attempt to "get in there" with Sally, she explores this model with the aid of a virtual reality glove and mask. One of the cards—with an image of a falling man, evidently from a Tarot pack—alerts Ruth to what Sally may be up to. At the peak of her helix, Sally has placed another Tarot card, with a picture of dogs baying at the crescent moon. Suddenly comprehending Sally's iconography of grief, Ruth forms a plan to erect a similar structure on her grounds, this one made of plywood and steel.

Sally has made a staircase to the moon, which represents her desire to move from "one home to another." Yet her construction, a mishmash of playing cards interspersed with family photographs, is literally a house of cards. It is inherently unstable, an imaginative home that no one can truly inhabit. The psychologist states the problem that Sally poses. Grudgingly he admits that there is something special about this child when he discovers her standing on a window ledge in his office playroom, hidden in plain sight against the bark of a tree outside, her body elaborately camouflaged by finger paints. "All right," he concedes, "that card castle of hers is a creative act. What she did on her skin is a work of art. Does a person withdraw from or return to the world through creativity? Very important question."

For me, withdrawal from the world did not so much involve creativity as anxiety. If I avoided social contact, it was because I didn't know how to behave and was afraid of making mistakes. Studying was a whole lot simpler. In the solitude of the library, I could lose myself in the world of books, where I felt safe. Like Sally, I was also immersed in a private fantasy of communion with my father. Although I did not expect to find him in the crescent moon, I tried to maintain a thread of connection by mirroring his intellectual achievements. How could he not appreciate my academic success?

In *House of Cards,* it is Ruth's effort to comprehend her daughter on her own terms that releases Sally from the death grip of her desire to join her father along with her eerie silence. Exhausted by her labors at the woodland construction site, Ruth falls asleep there one night. Meanwhile, Sally wanders out of the house in an attempt to get closer to the (now full) moon. Passing her mother at the bottom of the spiral, she starts to climb. Ruth, dreaming this very possibility, rises and follows, assuring Sally that she can accompany her. But the structure begins to wobble dangerously under Ruth's weight, causing her to fall and slide ignominiously back to the bottom, where she wakes with a start. Suddenly it is morning, and Sally has been discovered walking in the fields by her brother Michael and the equally sleepless psychologist, who has come to apologize to Ruth for treating her daughter as mentally ill. Ruth seizes on this opportunity to take Sally back to the spiral tower in order to demonstrate to her that it is strong enough to support them both. "I woke too soon," she says, implying an overlap or fusion between her dream and Sally's reality.

This time, Ruth ascends ahead of Sally, in an attempt to show her that it is safe.

"Watch, watch," she says urgently. "I can do it. We can do it together."

Sally gazes silently at her mother, communicating her desire in a whispered voice-over. Her father, she believes, is "all alone in the moon," and that is why she wants to join him.

"You can't go there," Ruth tells her.

"Show me," says Sally.

Not having witnessed her father's death, Sally has no conviction of its reality. Ruth, who has done her best to censor her own grief, making both her children "promise not to cry" in the immediate aftermath of the accident, now offers Sally her flashback memory of his fatal fall. Mother and daughter share this silent vision, making good on the Indian guide's explanation that people dream in order "to see things better." With the image of her father's fall now clearly fixed in her mind, Sally gazes upward toward the moon. Turning back to Ruth, she reaches her hand to her mother's face and, wiping a tear from her cheek, speaks her first audible word since returning home.

"Mommy."

"Oh, Sally," Ruth cries, "I was trying to get to you."

Unlike Sally, I did not succeed in capturing my mother's attention. Already somewhat reticent, I simply withdrew further into my fantasy world, mostly composed of books. Luckily or unluckily, I had found a socially sanctioned means of retreat. As a result, no one took notice of me. No one, including myself, understood that there was anything wrong.

When I first saw *House of Cards,* I was beginning to comprehend the magnitude of my loss. The scene where Ruth tries to persuade her daughter that she can follow her up the spiral tower spoke directly to my sense of loneliness and anguish. "She gets to have her mother," I whispered to myself.

Sally may miss her father, but she still has one parent who is passionately concerned for her well-being—enough to rescue her from her suicidal fascination with height. My own mother was too preoccupied with settling my father's estate in the weeks and months succeeding his death—and otherwise sunk in her grief—to offer comfort to me and my brothers.

It was as if we had all taken a vow of silence. Not only did we not speak the unspeakable, we showed no emotion in one another's presence. We didn't cry, hug, or try to console one another. Instead, we drew apart, the unacknowledged grief in our midst as vast and implacable as a glacier.

When I cried, as I did rarely in my young adult years, I didn't know why. One year, in graduate school, I wept at the sight of the sycamores, maples, and elms losing their leaves, feeling a profound sadness that I didn't know how to interpret.

I thought it was something universal that I felt. Lines from "Spring and Fall," a poem by Gerard Manley Hopkins, kept running through my mind. Addressed to a young child, this poem begins:

> Márgarét, are you gríeving
> Over Goldengrove unleaving?
> Leáves, like the things of man, you
> With your fresh thoughts care for, can you?

I appreciated Hopkins for taking seriously a little girl's tears, seeing in them—as I later saw in my daughter's questions about death—a sign of her awakening to mortality.

"Now no matter, child, the name:" the poem continues in a gently soothing tone.

> Sórrow's spríngs áre the same.
> Nor mouth had, no nor mind, expressed
> What heart heard of, ghost guessed:
> It ís the blight man was born for,
> It is Margaret you mourn for.

Hopkins's poem gives expression to feelings I was unable to articulate for myself. Like Margaret (or Sally) I could not fathom my own mourning. Although I thought I was crying for something as simple as the end of summer, I believe I was also crying for Anne and our dream of knowledge as a bulwark against life; for my mother, who was so unnerved by my dad's death that she could not attend to the grief of her children; and for my brothers, both of whom also suffered.

I was crying for the lives we all might have lived, for the little girl I once was and no longer knew how to reach. For the child so stunned into silence that the springs of her sorrow had no name.

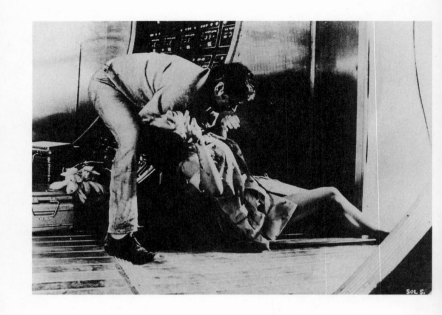

Repetition:

Solaris

> Time cannot vanish without trace for it is a subjec-
> tive, spiritual category. The time we have lived
> settles in our soul as an experience placed within
> time. In a certain sense the past is far more real, at
> any rate more stable, more resilient than the pres-
> ent. The present slips and vanishes like sand be-
> tween the fingers, acquiring material weight in
> its recollection.
>
> — Andrei Tarkovsky, *Sculpting in Time*

In SEPTEMBER OF 1977, I took a trip to England
by myself. My husband Frank and I had separated the year
before. I had fallen in love (one of the reasons for the separation), had had my heart broken, and wanted to do something
to prove my independence. Crossing an ocean seemed like a
good idea. I pictured this act as a pure leap into space, as if
I were jumping off the edge of the earth. "Flying over the
ocean," I wrote in my journal as I gazed out the window of
the plane, "seems like entering another world or visiting
another planet. I won't quite believe England exists until I
get there."

I am an anxious traveler. I worry about arriving at the airport too late, missing connections, not having hotel reservations, or making a fool of myself in front of strangers. For ten
years or so (the duration of my marriage), I rarely went any
place on my own. I told myself I was too busy teaching, taking care of my daughter, and writing critical articles so I

could get tenure, but the truth is I was scared. It was Frank who traveled, making frequent field trips with his 4 X 5 camera to make the photographs of grain elevators that were his passion at the time. I envied his ease and freedom of movement in the world. After we separated, I felt it was time to try my own wings.

On my return from England, my plane crossed over Greenland in the late afternoon, at a height of 30,000 feet. The sky was clear, and I could see all the way down to the water. I sat glued to the window, entranced by the view of the ocean, dotted with islands of ice. They seemed both beautiful and unreal to me, "like something in a science-fiction novel," I wrote in my journal, "or a fairy tale." A few weeks later, I persuaded my current boyfriend to take me and my eight-year-old daughter to see *Solaris*.

I didn't know anything about Andrei Tarkovsky. But something I had heard about this film must have intrigued me or I wouldn't have urged my distinctly "unartsy" lover to drive us out to the suburbs for this short-run feature. What I realized pretty quickly is that the film, confusing enough in itself, was nearly impossible for Jessica to follow through subtitles. Her whispered questions began to disturb not only my boyfriend but also the people around us, so we moved to the back of the theater. In this way, struggling to comprehend the enigmatic action and imagery of the film while offering a simultaneous translation to my daughter, I encountered Tarkovsky's rendition of the Polish science-fiction novel by Stanslaw Lem.

I fell in love with the opening imagery of grasses swaying gently underwater, set to the stately music of Bach's organ Prelude in F Minor. The camera lingers caressingly on this image, as if to make it ours, to imprint it on our memory. Like this opening "long take," the tempo of the film as a whole is leisurely, contemplative. In contrast to the typical fast-paced, plot-driven, sci-fi movie, Tarkovsky's exploration of Lem's otherworldly fiction withholds the gratification of quick response in favor of a nameless dis-ease and a brooding sense of inwardness. By refusing to locate us in the usual terms of time, space, and relationship, Tarkovsky takes us off guard, causing us to share the existential dilemma of his hero. We are in a strangely familiar and unfamiliar world from the very beginning of the film, struggling to get our bearings.

Gradually the plot line begins to emerge. Kris Kelvin, a psychologist, is on the point of leaving his parents' dacha to investigate the mysterious happenings on the Solaris space station. A report by the astronaut Burton reveals disturbing properties of the planet's ocean, which seems to induce hallucinations in those who come into its proximity. Kelvin must decide, on the course of his mission, whether to recommend abandoning years of research into the nature of this ocean.

Kelvin, who takes the opportunity to burn old papers while visiting his father's home, seems to have no close emotional ties—neither to father, wife, nor child. He seems isolated and sad as he takes his early morning walk in the autumn landscape. He has the air of a man who is surveying his past and setting his affairs in order, unsure that he will live to return.

Kelvin's remoteness and self-preoccupation are not accidental. He is a younger version of the father he now attempts, somewhat feebly, to make contact with before saying goodbye to Earth. As a result, he is completely unprepared for the experience that awaits him on the Solaris space station.

The planet Solaris consists primarily of ocean, a restless, plastic substance that is capable of creating islands with all of the features of Earth, as well as remarkably life-like beings.

The latter emerge, quite literally, from the dreaming minds of the inhabitants of the space station. Kris encounters evidence of these "visitors" on his arrival. The station, which now houses only two scientists (one having recently committed suicide), is in an obvious state of neglect. The two remaining men, Snaut and Sartorious, greet Kelvin with varying degrees of suspicion and hostility, attempting to conceal the presence of their "guests." Snaut evades Kelvin's rational queries and advises him to talk to him later—after he has taken a nap. Mystified and wary, Kelvin retreats to his room, the entrance to which he carefully barricades with two heavy trunks before falling asleep. When he wakes, he discovers a woman calmly seated across from his bed.

This woman, named Hari, knows Kris and greets him intimately. She appears to be his former wife, whom he abandoned years ago on Earth and who subsequently committed suicide. Kris is understandably unnerved, even panicked. His first action is deceptive and evasive. He persuades Hari to accompany him to the space shuttle room, where he first lures her into the capsule, then locks the door on her, and finally blasts her into the stratosphere. In his initial shock and terror, all he wants to do is get rid of her. Like a figure straight out of his unconscious, however, she rematerializes overnight. When Kelvin awakes, she is there, evidently unfazed, with no memory of her recent, traumatic departure.

As viewers, we are one step ahead of Kelvin in comprehending the bizarre nature of this occurrence. After Hari's second disappearance and return, we understand that Kelvin is reliving his own past. Yet this is no dream. Hari experiences herself as real, as does Kris. The emanation elicited from his memory by the Solaris Ocean is indistinguishable from a living, breathing human being. What happens to Kris is not just a replay of his former history. Rather, the events that take place on the Solaris station are a complex amalgam of the old and the new, a reliving of Hari's suicide—with a difference. Although Kris cannot reverse the trajectory of time or alter its tragic outcome, he has an opportunity to change his reaction to this painful memory.

When I flew to England I encountered much that was new, but, like Kelvin, I also flew straight into the heart of my past. Although I had never been to England before, I had a friend from graduate school who lived in London and who offered to put me up. I shared a small flat with Helen, her husband, and two young children, while touring the city on my own. Toward the end of my stay, Helen offered to host a dinner party for me, which she planned around the theme of American expatriates. It would include four guests in addition to Helen and her architect husband—all of whom had chosen to make their home abroad. One, a female writer from the South, was coming with her Detroit-born, black, fashion-designer lover. The other couple, a publisher and a cabaret-singer, had once lived in St. Louis, where I grew up. Despite the St. Louis connection, I felt like a country cousin in relation to my New York friend Helen and her sophisticated London social set. During cocktails, my worst fears were borne out. Surrounded by witty conversation, including references to the latest books, plays, and music, I felt ignorant and tongue-tied.

Over dinner, a complicated osso bucco recipe, prepared and served with flair by my friend Helen, I turned to my seatmate Jay, in an effort to make conversation.

"Helen tells me you're from St. Louis," I said. "Where did you live?"

"In the West End," Jay said, turning toward me with interest. "I used to own an antique store in Gaslight Square. Do you know that area?"

As it happens, I did know something about Gaslight

Square, a district that had been transformed sometime in the late 1950s and early '60s by an influx of coffee houses and nightclubs, which supported a lively folk, blues, and jazz scene. It was a place where you could participate in discussions of Camus and Sartre, hear Beat poetry read, or listen to the local longhairs play political protest songs. To me as a teenager, growing up in a sheltered, middle-class neighborhood, it was a place that felt a little dangerous, a little wild.

"Yes, I know where that is," I said. "My dad used to shop there for antiques. He made seismographs for a living, but he loved antiques and liked to browse."

"What's your name?" Jay asked.

"Sprengnether. It's a bit unusual." I spelled it for him.

"I used to know a man by that name," Jay said slowly. "He came around a lot, and I sold him some things. The biggest item was a crystal chandelier."

"What was it like?"

"Very elaborate, very ornate. It came from a hotel that had been torn down in Chicago. Lots of cut glass. Heavy, too. It was something special."

I knew the chandelier Jay was talking about. It was one of the truly magical objects from my childhood. I remembered how it caught the sunlight in its myriad facets, casting tiny, dancing rainbows around our dining room. The day my dad brought it home flashed into mind. He was so excited that he wanted to hang it right away. When he had finally gotten it fixed to the ceiling, he wrapped red velvet ribbon around the thick chain. I loved that chandelier. If anything could represent true happiness—the time in my childhood when I felt most at peace and secure in the world—it was that glittering, prismatic object.

"You're talking about my father," I said.

"He was interested in everything," Jay continued. "I liked him. He wasn't what I would call sophisticated, but he had style. You know, my wife Fran keeps telling me not to talk about St. Louis. She doesn't want to go back. But I had a good time in those days. I wouldn't mind living there again."

I followed Jay's eyes as he glanced down the table to see if Fran was taking any notice of us. She wasn't.

"I remember your mother, too," Jay confided. "She was a beautiful woman, but also reserved. Very dignified. She didn't have much of a sense of humor. I used to like to tease her—nothing serious, just a little flirt. But I couldn't get a rise out of her."

"That sounds like my mother."

"What happened to him? Wasn't there some . . . accident?"

"We had a boat," I said, projected suddenly into another landscape, where I saw myself standing on a strip of beach with my mother and two brothers, trying to hail a passing speedboat for help. I took a deep breath and lurched into the only narrative I knew for the unspeakable thing that had occurred—the story my brother Bob told me, sometime in my thirties, when I finally summoned the courage to ask.

"What about your brother?" Jay asked when I had finished, now completely absorbed in our one-on-one conversation.

"My mother pulled him out. By the time I understood what was happening, it was over—my dad was gone."

More fragments of this story began to fly out of me—like shrapnel.

"My dad had a friend whose name was Al Hunt. He came to get the boat. We left it at the nearest town on the river when we went to get help. We spent the afternoon in some-body's trailer and flew back to St. Louis in a private airplane. Al sold the boat for us. I never saw it again."

What difference did it make about the boat? Or the chandelier? But we still had the chandelier—hanging in the house my mother and stepfather had bought, in our new dining room. With no red ribbon wound around the chain and no Southern light to flash through its shining, crystal pendants.

Later that evening, we smoked dope—Helen's husband's idea. He had a huge stash of some powerful homegrown stuff that he wanted to try out. Sitting on the floor, silent and Buddha-like, he passed several rounds. At some point in this already unsettling evening, I began to feel oddly porous, or permeable. I felt that I was hearing every nuance in the conversation, every subtle, unspoken thing in the relations among us. The writer, who seemed so worldly-wise, was suddenly anxious. I sensed that she was unsure of her young, black lover. Both, in the course of the evening, were drawn to stories from their childhood—she to memories of the smell of hardwood floors in a neighborhood drugstore, he to the mean streets of Detroit. My friend Helen embarked on a long, novelistic narrative about a trip to Italy—with Jay, the publisher, as enthusiastic audience, offering to make her rich and famous. Fran talked, seemingly oblivious to Jay's presence, about the necessity of feminine accommodation to a man's world.

Helen's husband and I were the silent ones. While he seemed too meditative, morose, or just plain stoned to talk, I felt overwhelmed by the symphony of voices around me. I was lifted temporarily out of myself, as if I were some kind of recorder or receiving device. I felt full of their awkward, cacophonous, and painful stories—as much as my own. Toward the end of the evening, we each descended into a dope craving for sweetness—for dark chocolate, ice cream, and other sensual delights. A hunger for some representation of inner content, drawn from the depths of our individual histories. Like my memory of the crystal chandelier, or the writer's longing for the smell of sawdust on wood floors.

After I had seen *Solaris,* I associated the view of the ocean over Greenland with Tarkovsky's watery planet. Restless, undulant, and ultimately unknowable, Tarkovsky's ocean fascinated and terrified me. As with the unsuspecting Kris Kelvin, it began to fuse with my dreaming mind. Within a day or two of seeing *Solaris,* I had a dream about flying to the moon and walking on its benign, crystalline surface, while watching the stars revolve overhead, as if the universe were my private planetarium. Later, though, I had a more disturbing dream, which reminded me of the painful interaction between Kelvin and his uncanny female companion. In this dream, I was making love with a man named "Burton"—the name of the discredited space scientist in *Solaris,* but also the name (according to a newspaper account) of a man who threw lye in the face of his estranged girlfriend. At this point, I realized how unnerved I had been by the plot of *Solaris,* especially by its portrayal of the love relation between Kris and Hari, which reminded me uncomfortably of parts of my own romantic history.

When Kris goes away, Hari dies—literally, in film terms. She must keep Kris within sight, she says, though she doesn't know why. When he leaves her to visit Snaut, closing the door of their room behind him, she goes into a panic, hurling herself against its shiny metal surface. Horrified, Kris watches as she beats her body against the door, tearing through it and fatally wounding herself in the process. Kris carries her back into the bedroom, where slowly she revives, the lacerations on her body healing before his very eyes. When she wakes, she has no memory of having "died." As before, she is oblivious to what has happened. Snaut explains these "resurrections," pointing out that they intensify as they repeat themselves. Each death becomes more painful to undergo, each return more excruciating to observe. Although the Solaris Hari is not real in human terms, she carries the Earth

Hari's history and must experience it as if it were her own. With Kris as captive witness.

Watching this film, I began to feel like a captive witness myself, wishing I had not insisted on seeing it, and especially regretting that I had brought Jessica, whose mystification increased at each new turn of the plot. I guess I could have left the theater, but the fact that I was sitting apart from my boyfriend, who had not wanted to move his seat, prevented me. Also, I rarely leave a movie. Some need for narrative resolution keeps my eyes riveted to the screen. In this case, no matter how awful it might be, I wanted to know what would happen next. I had to see how it all turned out.

As Snaut predicts, things do get worse. At first Hari "dies" when Kris leaves her—blasting her off in the space shuttle or simply closing the door between them. Later, like her Earth counterpart, she resolves to take her own life. As Hari begins to comprehend her status as nonhuman, she also starts to despair. Loving Kris as she does, yet unable to bear his absence, she decides to kill herself. She finds and swallows the contents of a canister of liquid oxygen, which burns through her internal organs, leaving her body arched and rigid. When Kris discovers her, she is already dead, her body frosted with ice crystals. By now, Kris knows the story; there is nothing he can do but wait until she recovers. Resigned to the pain of this spectacle, he sits by her, as slowly her body warms, melting her frozen shirt. In the most arresting scene of the film, Hari "convulses" back to life. This is no miracle healing, but rather a torment. Hari cannot choose not to live. She is condemned to her anguish, which we witness in purely physical terms, as a series of involuntary seizures rack her body back to breath and motion.

Hari's spasms, which seem to rise from someplace in her lower abdomen, ripple upward through her chest and back, lifting her whole torso off the floor. They pass through her in waves, contracting her facial muscles and forcing guttural sounds from her throat. She is only half dressed, wearing Kris's nightshirt, which clings to her body, revealing the outline of her breasts and nipples. If we did not know what was happening, we might think she was having a hysterical breakdown or experiencing a particularly powerful orgasm. It is the erotic edge to this scene that makes it so disturbing.

The movie had an unusual effect on me. On the way home, I felt a series of spontaneous contractions in my vulva—little pulses of pleasure that didn't add up to a climax, but hovered somewhere in the vicinity. I enjoyed this sensation, which lasted for quite some time, but had no idea what provoked it. I had never felt anything like this before in response to a film, and nothing of the kind has happened since. Like my dream about making love with the man named Burton, it seemed keyed to my viewing of *Solaris*.

I tried to untangle this web of feelings and associations. What does the story of the man who threw lye in his girlfriend's face have to do with the death of Hari, I wondered? One is an act of violent retribution, the other an act of self-inflicted harm. "What is the connection?" I wrote in my journal. "Could it be an association between pleasure and being hurt?" Despite the obvious differences between these two stories, they share a common theme. Love, in both, is inseparable from pain.

Once in a while, when I have a very intense orgasm, I find myself crying. It's as though any powerful physiological reaction, whether pleasurable or painful, triggers a whole body response. Is this a purely muscular phenomenon? Or something more liminal? Suppose our bodies are wired in such a way that we cannot experience an emotion without a corresponding physical sensation? Suppose our bodies are the repositories of our cumulative feeling states? A carnal memory bank, so to speak.

In the fall of 1977, I was musing on the mind-body connection, much as I did in the aftermath of seeing *Pather Panchali*. But I had no framework for these thoughts, and they scared me. I was afraid that loving fully, with the effort of the whole self, also involved some form of violence or self-annihilation. If I loved like Hari, would I share her fate?

When my father died, it was as though he simply vanished. At first, I refused to believe he was actually gone. He was so real, so vital, so important to me. He couldn't just disappear like that—into thin air, like smoke. Surely this was some kind of elaborate deception or trick. For years, I played variations on the fantasy that he had been called away on a secret government mission—which might help to make sense of the silence surrounding his funeral and why we never talked about him in my family. One part of me understood that he was dead, while another part wanted desperately to believe that he would someday return. I had regular dreams about this. In one, he had gone to South America, where I joined him in a lush, semi-tropical setting and swam beside him in a blue lagoon, matching him stroke for stroke, like Esther Williams. Dreams like this were visitations, which made me happy for a time. They relieved my underlying sense of despair. Gradually, however, I grew out of them. Then the future stretched ahead of me like a nuclear wasteland, ashy and bleak.

For years, the color washed out of my life. I no longer lived in gleaming Technicolor, but in gritty, neo-realist black and white. I was well into my first psychotherapy before my world began to brighten up. I remember this moment distinctly, because it reminded me of the way that Dorothy, in Frank Baum's classic tale, wakes from her dreary Kansas home into the richly hued and magical land of Oz. This sensation was so powerful that I wanted to protect it. I felt that I had stumbled on a secret door at the back of a closet that leads into a wonderland of adventure. But, like Oz, this new world held hidden dangers. It was a place of pleasure and excitement, but it was also a place of threat. By deadening myself, I had made my life relatively safe and predictable. Now that I had a fuller range of emotional color, I was faced with more choices, more hazards, more opportunities for making mistakes. Falling in love was just such a zone of peril.

The trouble with my first marriage was that I hadn't fallen in love. I had started to, but then stopped. I let myself go a certain distance and then froze. I sensed that there was something more I ought to be feeling, but was unsure what this might be. I knew there was a missing element—in the relationship or in myself—but couldn't give shape in my imagination to an experience I had never had. Except perhaps as a child, in the wholehearted way I had loved my father. This model seemed useless to me, however, as an adult. When I did fall wildly and passionately in love with a man in my mid-thirties, I was unprepared for the fury of emotion I felt, which lifted me off the ground, like the tornado that rips Dorothy's house from its moorings, slamming me down in a totally unfamiliar landscape.

I felt every nuance of romantic fantasy and desire that had escaped me as an early teenager and adolescent. Unimmunized by the milder strains of love, I suffered it in a virulent form. I had no slowly acquired practical wisdom to guide me, no healthy realism, no structures of defense. I was ignorant of the inner world of myself, which, like the Solaris Ocean, was sentient and mysterious—a little chaos seething with equal powers of creation and destruction.

When I first discovered this hidden space in myself, I was startled by its intense reactivity. Which "me" was real, I wondered, the responsible wife, mother, and university professor, or this other creature—a prey to firebrand emotions, like Bertha Mason in Charlotte Brontë's *Jane Eyre*. I was frightened by this volatile and unknown self, but once she had come out of hiding, I was unable to give her up. She was a "wild child" of sorts, ferocious and barely articulate, as likely to bite and scratch as to express gratitude for a kindness. Yet I was sure that her destiny, however painful or disruptive, was also mine.

The man I loved only half-loved me. We came together over our mutual love of literature, spending hour after hour in rapt conversation. When we began to touch, it seemed the natural extension of our verbal interaction. But I was married, and he was living with someone else. Any fool could have told me what I was in for, but I was driven by a kind of compulsion that no clear-eyed realism can assuage.

Somehow we managed to conceal our passion (even our furtive sexual encounters) from our respective partners for several months. At this point, my lover abruptly broke off with me by announcing publicly that he was going to marry his girlfriend. A woman with a cooler head in my circumstances would have been able to feign an attitude of congratulation. But I was shocked to the core of my newly aroused and vulnerable sexual self. I couldn't hide my dismay. I forced a confrontation, in which I yelled, threatened, and finally (infuriated by my lover's seeming imperviousness) slapped him on the face. I hit him with such force that I knocked his glasses off, which only upset me more. Hitting someone with glasses was a violation of all the childhood rules of a fair fight. It was about as low as you could get.

Words leapt out of my mouth before I could stop them. I said things I didn't mean but couldn't retract. I wanted to cut off his hands, I said. I wanted to burn down his house. Where did such rage come from? I sounded like a madwoman or some kind of terrorist. If this was love, it was excruciating, like having barbed wire wrapped around your heart.

My marriage, somewhat shaky from the beginning, collapsed around the spectacle of my rage and grief. I was simply unable to lie to my husband about my state of mind. This was not a matter of choice. I had never, in my adult life, endured such a loss. It knocked me flat.

Despite the illicit nature of our relationship, I didn't understand how my lover could sever our connection so coldly, with no warning. It was like a sudden failure of electricity, plunging me into internal darkness. For a few weeks, I barely functioned, doing only what I had to in order to get through the day. My husband was oddly gentle with me at this time. Perhaps he could not bear to make my readily observable suffering any worse. It wasn't until much later, when I began to feel better, that he left. In the meantime, I oscillated between states of listlessness, driving anger, and grief. I was on some terrifying roller coaster of myself, which I couldn't get off.

I used to fear that, somewhere underneath my façade of dutiful responsibility, I was actually crazy. My inner world— to the extent that I thought about it—seemed messy and disorganized, like the wildly scribbled lines of a drawing by Willem de Kooning, complete with a staring-eyed, disjointed woman. The loss of my first grown-up love liberated this frenetic self, who seemed to run in circles, in a panic at her sudden freedom. But she wasn't psychotic; she didn't hallucinate, hear voices, or construct elaborate conspiracy theories. She was just angry and hurt. Gradually, she calmed down enough for me to attend to her anguish. I began to put my ear to her heart.

There ought to be a word in our vocabulary for the opposite of "exorcism," for the process of welcoming back a self one has tried to disown or expel. Like any neglected child, such a self is difficult, unruly, and unkempt. She is not easy to love. At first, it was all I could do to acknowledge her presence, to allow her into the same room with me. I wanted her to wash her hands or comb her hair first. But she refused; she had her own agenda, and she meant to push it for all it was worth. Even now, when I feel that my life is in an order I don't want to disrupt, I sometimes pretend I have never seen her before—that we are not related. When this happens, she is likely to throw a fit, overturning the careful chess game I am trying to play or sweeping the cards onto the floor.

This *enfant terrible,* through her passionate demands, made a shambles of my first marriage. She forced a dark looking glass into my hands. Like an unsuspecting Alice, I walked through it into a topsy-turvy landscape, where at long last I began to explore the topography of grief. All the emotions I had displaced as a child were there waiting for me, as wrenching and real as they were when I closed the door on them at age nine.

When I looked at Hari, who felt she could not survive out of contact with her beloved, yet who kept reviving herself after her own death, I saw some remote, yet powerfully resonant version of myself. For years, I had had dreams of a woman in a coma or a state of anaphylactic shock whom I must bring back to life. In these dreams, I was both victim and rescuer, the one near death and the one who offers help. But I didn't see the connection. Like Kris, my first reactions were ones of flight. Now, suddenly, the figure/ground field reversed. While I was certainly Kris reliving his past, I was more fundamentally Hari, struggling to maintain her autonomy, some minimal form of identity or self.

Falling in love, I think, revives our deepest memories of being cared for when we were small. All the things we cannot remember, but which remain somatically embedded in our bodies, return. Whether it was easy or difficult to take nourishment, relax, or to sleep. Whether or not we felt secure in being watched over or cherished. Whether our wordless expressions of need (for food, physical comfort, or being held) were met. The loss of love in adult experience touches all of these sensitive nerve centers. It makes us relive the unresolved losses of our earliest lives.

When I fell in love in my mid-thirties, I also fell down the well of my past. At the bottom of this steep shaft I discovered black emotions, the existence of which I hadn't suspected, a moil of sorrow and frenzy I could no longer ignore, much less shrug off. When my lover left me, I felt panicky and unreal. While I was with him, I felt self-confident, even at times euphoric, but when he departed I didn't quite know who I was. Like Hari, I seemed to need contact in order to feel grounded in myself. The awakening of my passionate, loving self had opened a world of intense feeling, but it had also projected me into a space of solitude that felt like emptiness. When I first began to notice this inner void in myself, I tried to intellectualize it—as if I might find comfort in the company of philosophers who had preceded me into this territory. I thought about Bishop Berkeley and the conundrum of the tree falling in the forest. Does it make a sound if no one is there to hear? To be is to be perceived, Berkeley concluded, and I pretty much agreed. I needed someone to notice me in order to feel like myself. When I lost the mirror of my lover's adoring regard, I lost some piece of my interior reality.

Even in 1977, I was aware of the connection between this state of mind and the disappearance of my father. Writing in my journal about Hari's inability to sustain herself in the absence of her lover, I noted: "When Kris leaves, Hari dies— is this my fear about my dad's death?" Although I had survived this trauma, I had not permitted myself to feel its full impact. Not falling in love was a kind of emotional insurance policy I signed with myself. As long as I did not make myself vulnerable to grief, I would not have to experience its devastating effects. But the rules of the game had changed—by my own choice.

I took a step, the impact of which I could not gauge, then suffered its consequences. I could see all of this happening before my eyes in Hari's ecstasy of pain. For me, as for her, love was both compulsion and torment. Having such a limited exposure to passion, I didn't know how it could be otherwise. A love like this seemed something to avoid, a sickness or pathology.

I wondered if I was drawn only to men who would leave me or whether the kind of intensity of connection I sought was somehow wrong in itself. Yet I couldn't give it up. I persisted in wanting my lover back and continued to seek him out. His own ambivalence was such that he responded from time to time—just enough to keep me hoping. I wanted to believe that he would come back. We kept repeating the pattern of our first rupture—coming together with magnetic force, then just as violently ripping apart. I maintained this punishing cycle until some strength of will I didn't know I had allowed me to end it. I took myself in hand and forced a conclusion. My feelings didn't really resolve themselves, but out of desperation and exhaustion, I made them stop.

For years after my final breakup with my lover, I thought of this relationship as serving my need to grieve my father's death. The reason it went on so long, I told myself, is that it took this length of time (five years altogether) for me to plumb the depths of my sorrow. While this is surely true, I think there is another, equally powerful truth embedded in this experience. Each time my lover left, it felt like a death to me—to which I reacted with all the pent-up feelings I had had as a child. I cried, I raged, I went into a temporary downward spiral of depression. In this state, I questioned my ability to lead my life with any future pleasure or happiness. Some part of me lost heart; some part of me was dying. Yet, in the midst of this suffering, I clung to the fantasy that things would still work out. I would fan the flame of this desire until the force of attraction between me and my lover brought us back into each other's orbit. Although the deep structure of our relationship never altered, I continued to believe that it might. I couldn't bear to extinguish this hope. In this way, I not only relived the pain of my father's loss, I also sustained my childish faith that he would come back. No wonder I was moved by the spectacle of Hari's expiring and coming back to life; I had been trapped in a similarly excruciating cycle of loss.

As an adult woman, I had long ago given up the notion that my dad had slipped away on a top-secret mission. He was dead and buried—I knew that. In each man I was passionately attracted to, however, I sought some aspect of him. He would return to me, I felt, in the form of a lover. In this way, I could believe that he was not forever lost. While I had the strength to end my tempestuous five-year affair, eventually finding a more satisfying relationship in my second marriage, I did not relinquish the fantasy of someone who would embody my father's all-encompassing love. I still did not want to let him go.

In 1977, I was so transfixed by the drama of Hari's death and resurrection that I could barely attend to the film's denouement. A full seventeen years passed before I saw it again. During this interval, I forgot the whole last section, the part where Kris comes to terms with his past, reconciling himself with his parents as well as his former wife. In this lyrical phase, Kris enters a dreamlike state in which he visits his Earth home, encountering phantom figures of his mother and his wife, who become imagistically interchangeable.

Toward the end of this sequence, his mother bathes his arm in a white basin—as earlier Kris had bathed Hari's lacerated arm. When he wakes, Hari is gone. With Snaut's help, she has managed to dematerialize herself permanently. The other space station "guests" have similarly vanished. Now the mysterious Solaris Ocean is forming islands, Snaut says. It is time for Kelvin to go home.

In revisiting his past, Kris has discovered a new love for Hari—not the woman he once brutally abandoned, but her Solaris double. After his first attempt to eject this "Hari" from the space station (as he has tried to expel other disturbing memories from his childhood), he chooses to embrace her, honoring her love and vulnerability, including her obsessive need for his presence. On a psychological level, you might say that Kris is finally able to forgive himself and Hari for their mutually tragic history. This melting of resistance then opens a path of reconciliation between Kris and his parents—both his long-lost mother and his emotionally distant father. At the very end of the film, Kris returns to his father's dacha, slowly approaching the house and peering into a window, where it is raining inside. He goes to the front door, and as his father appears, falls on his knees, embracing him.

On what level does this resolution occur? Does Kris really return to Earth, or is this just another phantasm elicited from his dreaming mind? As the camera pulls back from this scene, we see the dacha situated on one of the newly formed islands of the Solaris Ocean. In the world of science fiction, nothing and everything is real. In Tarkovsky's private film vocabulary, the phenomenon of interior rain indicates something like mercy, hence signaling a shift in Kris's emotional state. By this point, the truth value of the action is not at issue. It is Kris's inner journey that accounts for the film's trajectory, giving it a feeling of satisfying completion.

How could I forget such a powerful ending, especially in

view of my need to see the film through? My guess is that I remembered most vividly only the scenes that spoke to me personally. What I could not picture as a form of resolution for myself, I literally could not retain in my memory. I was too bound to my own inner drama of love and loss to imagine a time when I might feel release. Love, I thought, was inherently painful, an exquisite form of suffering, to which the only alternative was numbness or indifference. If you want the full experience of passion, I believed, this is the price you have to pay.

Will
1993–1994

Will:

The Piano

> Shall will in others seem right gracious,
> And in my will no fair acceptance shine?
>
> ⸺ William Shakespeare, Sonnet 135

Wʜᴇɴ ɪ sᴀᴡ *ᴛʜᴇ ᴘɪᴀɴᴏ* in the fall of 1993, I felt that my life was settled. Ten years before I had fallen in love and remarried. In the meantime, my daughter had grown up, moved away from home, and graduated from college. After a stormy period during her adolescence, we were on good terms. I was happy with my husband and overall liked my life. Or so I believed. Jane Campion's *The Piano* upset this careful balance, reminding me of impulses and desires I had done my best to suppress, while setting the stage for a new series of upheavals in my life.

It was rainy and blustery on the day I went to see this film, an atmosphere appropriate to its watery coloration and feeling of emotional undertow. I knew next to nothing about Campion, whose only other work I'd seen was *Sweetie,* a quirky tale of two sisters, one of whom dies, a quasi-suicide. I was unprepared for the greater sophistication of *The Piano,* which presents itself as a nineteenth-century period drama. I was also unprepared for the frankness, even violence, of its eroticism. I became mesmerized by this story of a furiously silent woman and her id-like drama of will.

The Piano begins with a voice-over in which the protagonist Ada, who is otherwise mute, speaks directly to the audience.

"The voice you hear," she warns, "is not my speaking voice, but my mind's voice." She has not spoken since she was six years old, for reasons even she does not know. "My father says it is a dark talent," she continues, "and the day I take it into my head to stop breathing will be my last." Ada does communicate, but in nonverbal ways—through looks, signing, writing on a pad she carries suspended from her neck, and through her piano playing.

For Ada, the piano is her chief means of expression, her disturbingly passionate "voice," described by one of the Scottish immigrants to New Zealand as "strange, like a mood that passes into you." Yet she does not share this voice with just anyone, often refusing to play or stopping abruptly when she senses an intruder. Ada's piano is an alter ego, her playing a form of intense communion with herself. Until the arrival of Baines, her husband Stewart's overseer, the only person allowed into this closed circuit is Flora, who sings, and sometimes plays duets, with her mother.

Flora's father has long since vanished from the scene. All we know of him is that he had been Ada's music instructor, with whom she felt she "didn't need to speak," being able to "lay thoughts out in his mind like they were a sheet" until he "stopped listening." They never married. In his absence, Flora invents a highly colored drama of her parents' musical career as opera singers, culminating in her father's tragic death by lightning in the midst of a thunderstorm. The truth is, Flora is happy to have her mother to herself, insisting on their arrival from Scotland to the New Zealand bush that she will never call her stepfather "Papa."

I knew how Flora felt. After my own father's death, I wanted no one to take his place. He had died at the height of my adoration of him, and I could not imagine anyone stepping into his shoes. Nor could I imagine the reality of my mother's life—

deprived of the emotional and economic support on which she had relied absolutely. My child's-eye view of the world governed my reactions to her remarriage—much as Flora is driven to prevent interference into her exclusive relationship with her mother.

My mother was not mute, but she was stubbornly silent on the subject of my father's death. We talked about him so little that he seemed hardly to have existed. My father was as much a phantom of my imagination as Flora's, a ghostly, yet romantic, figure who commanded my absolute fidelity. I wasn't about to transfer my longing for paternal love onto a complete stranger, much less a man whose physical appearance and personality were so much the opposite of my dad's.

Where my father was dark-eyed, curly-haired, sociable, and affectionate, a talker and a toucher, Victor was pale in every respect—from his washed-out complexion, light brown eyes, and silvery hair to his physical ill-at-easeness, his shy and awkward manner. Although previously married, Victor had no children of his own and was pretty much at a loss as to how to relate to me and my two brothers. I believe that he meant well by us, the chief sign of which was his sending us all to private schools, but this one gesture seemed to exhaust his notion of fatherhood. Later, on learning that he himself had lost his father at an early age, I felt compassion for him. Neither of us had received much guidance in growing up. For Victor, this meant that his manhood—including his attempt to play the part of a father—was something of a sham. At age thirteen when I was first introduced to him, I could hardly begin to imagine how difficult it must have been for him to enter a grieving family, much less to become an instant head of household. All I knew is that I hated him.

Very little in Ada's relationship with Flora changes at the outset of her marriage. Flora's role as her mother's interpreter assures the primacy of her bond, imaged by the tight circle of Ada's hoop skirt, which serves as a primitive shelter their first night on the beach. Infuriated by Stewart's refusal to have her piano transported with her other baggage to the house, Ada holds herself aloof from him, communicating, when necessary, in staccato bursts of signing. A husband in name only, Stewart is clearly no competitor for Ada's love. It is Flora she chooses to sleep with, sharing the physical warmth of her body along with the intimacy of her thoughts. With nothing to fear from Stewart, Flora accepts the new order of her life, obediently carrying wood from the chopping block and eagerly embracing her role as angel in the community theater play. As long as her mother shows no interest in a man other than her phantom father, Flora is content.

Enter Baines.

Baines's fascination with Ada's piano playing on the beach leads him to negotiate a trade of land for the piano with Stewart. He wishes to learn to play the instrument, he says, while insinuating that he will need instruction. The land-hungry Stewart agrees to this bargain, throwing in the services of his wife as teacher to sweeten the deal. From the first lesson, it is clear that Baines's interest is erotic. Sensing the importance to Ada of her piano, he makes her a proposition. One lesson—including her compliance with his instructions to disrobe—per black key. By surrendering to Baines's desire to watch her play in increasing stages of undress, she may win her instrument back. This is clearly an adult negotiation, from which Flora must be excluded. The combination of Flora's resistance to this sudden change of affairs and Stewart's awakened desire and rage leads to violence.

Although my family did not openly grieve my father's death, we did find ways to comfort ourselves. My brothers, who shared a bedroom, had each other's physical presence to take the edge off of their nighttime anxieties and fears. That left my mother and me isolated in our separate rooms and double beds, a hallway apart. It wasn't long before my mother invited me to sleep with her—an offer I tacitly understood. Through the warmth and proximity of our bodies, we would alleviate each other's loneliness. No matter what happened during the raw daytime hours, we would have this haven of intimacy to shelter us at night. Unlike Ada and Flora, we didn't tell stories or share a private language. We didn't even snuggle up to each other much. If we touched, it was more by accident than design. The consolation I received in this way, though limited to an awareness of my mother's presence through the dark hours of my sleep, was real, but fraught with the weight of unexpressed need. Sleeping with my mother was all that stood between me and the tidal wave of my sorrow.

Victor altered the fragile truce I had achieved with my grief. It's no wonder that I hated him as I did. My brothers and I went so far as to invent a secret society, which we named the VHA, standing for "Victor Haters Association." This society had no business and never met. Its reason for being was contained in its name. When my mother learned of its existence by pressuring my younger brother into a confession, she was understandably angry. The VHA went underground.

I had no say in my mother's decision to remarry. Although she once asked me what I thought of Victor, I knew that she had already made up her mind. I couldn't tell her how much I abhorred the idea of her bringing an outsider into our house. Unlike Flora, who makes an alliance with Stewart in an attempt to ward off Baines, I took no real action. Instead, I fumed in silence. Outwardly compliant, I was inwardly enraged.

I studiously ignored the preparations for the wedding—a private ceremony in a chapel on a weekday morning, attended only by the immediate family—while sinking slowly into a feeling of hopelessness. From this time forward, I could no longer pretend that my father would return to reclaim his place. If he came back now, he would find another man in his bed. As crazy as I understood this idea to be, I clung to it as the last remnant of my connection to him, my last chance to salvage something of our ruined past. My mother, who had once loudly proclaimed that she would never marry again, was now set to betray this promise. She was about to betray my dad, who must be waiting for her somewhere in the land of the dead. She was about to betray us all.

When Ada begins playing the piano for Baines in his cabin, she resolutely shuts the door on Flora, who tries to amuse herself by playing on the porch, but can't resist the temptation to peek through a knothole to see what is going on inside. Her glimpse of Ada and Baines reclining nude on his bed jolts her into a new kind of awareness, which she acts out with her Maori playmates in a game that involves hugging, caressing, and kissing trees. Stewart, who is shocked by this imitation of adult sexual play, reprimands Flora, claiming that she has shamed both herself and the trees. In penance, she is forced to scrub their trunks. Flora retaliates by betraying her mother's secret. Baines never plays the piano himself, she reveals. Her mother "just plays what she pleases, sometimes she doesn't play at all." His suspicions aroused, Stewart decides to investigate. His action is forestalled by Baines's abrupt conclusion of the piano lessons and return of the instrument to Ada. Unhappy that Ada does not reciprocate his passion, Baines explains to her that their bargain "is making you a whore and me wretched."

Flora's growing awareness of her mother's sexuality dovetails with Ada's gradual arousal of desire for Baines. The intersection of these two stories precipitates an act of violence reminiscent of the ax murder threatened in the amateur performance of *Bluebeard,* which so shocks the young Maori warriors in the audience that they rush to the stage to intervene. This grisly tale of a man who marries, then beheads a series of wives, eerily prefigures the course of Stewart's jealous rage—down to the ax he wields in threatening Ada.

The violence that erupts in *The Piano* shook me, reminding me of the violent conclusion of my mother's second marriage. And my virulent hatred. Victor had been responsible for my losing the only form of intimacy I had with my mother. In retaliation, I vividly imagined his death. We would be so much better off without him, I thought. If he died, we could go back to the way we were—an isolated, grieving family, but one that was at least bound by its experience of loss.

I pictured his departure as sudden. Because he traveled on business, I thought that an airplane crash would be convenient. Someday he would take a trip from which he would not return. We would be rid of him this way, without any of the mess or emotional turmoil of a death in our midst. Failing to comprehend the roots of my childhood resentment against my stepfather, I regularly plotted murder in my heart.

When Flora betrays her mother for a second time, she is desperate. Without comprehending the exact nature of her mother's attachment to Baines, she understands it as a threat. When Stewart boards up the house, claiming his wife as his property by barring the door from the outside, Flora sides with him. Stewart is her ally in her war against Baines. She is so in tune with Stewart that she takes to wearing her cast-off angel wings, while amusing herself with playing at household chores. When Stewart relents and unboards the house, freeing Ada to send a message to Baines inscribed on one of the keys from her piano, Flora at first refuses to act as go-between, then decides to deliver it to Stewart. While Flora is ignorant of the love declaration inscribed on the key, she senses that the gift will disrupt the domestic order she cherishes. Seeking to forestall this possibility, she disobeys her mother's instructions, betraying her to the man most likely to do her harm. Helplessly, she watches the drama of Stewart's fury unfold. Unlike the Maori warriors who rise up to protect Bluebeard's wife, she cannot prevent the painful spectacle she is forced to witness.

It is unclear at first what kind of violence Stewart intends. At an earlier point in the film when he drags Ada away from the path to Baines's house, he tries to rape her, assuming that he has as much right to enjoy her as Baines. Only the sudden appearance of Flora stops him. This time, his jealousy turns from lust to rage. Stewart's image in profile, with ax in hand against the sky, recalls the silhouette of Bluebeard about to commit an act of wife murder. But this is no shadow play. We are free to imagine the worst as Stewart bursts into the house and sinks his ax first into a table where Ada is quietly reading a book and then, with even greater force, into her piano. "Why do you do this?" he shouts. "Why do you make me hurt you? Do you hear? Why have you done it?" Finally, in frustration at her silence, he seizes her by the wrist and pulls her, struggling violently, to the wood block. When she breaks free and tries to crawl away, he grabs her by her hair and pulls her back. Everything in his words and behavior suggests that he is going to kill her. What he actually does is no less shocking. He chops off the index finger of her right hand.

Flora, who tries to protect her mother by screaming "NOOOOOO!!!" to Stewart's insistent questions, "Do you love him? Do you? Is it him you love?" stands by in anguish as her mother's blood spurts onto her white pinafore and angel wings. Later, Stewart sends her to Baines with the dead finger wrapped in the napkin that was intended to deliver the piano key. The bloody message, this time, is loud and clear: "He says you're not to see her or he'll chop her up!"

Flora's anguish and remorse mirrored my own in relation to Victor. At the height of my feelings of powerlessness and exclusion, I had wished him dead. But in time, as I adjusted to my new reality, I forgot about this wish. A few years into her marriage, when it became apparent that my mother was unhappy to the point of considering a divorce, I surprised myself by feeling upset. Wasn't this what I had wanted all along? All of a sudden, it wasn't. Victor's presence helped us to achieve a semblance of normalcy as a family, which gave me a feeling of security, if not love. A figurehead father, I decided, was better than none. I was heartsick at the thought of a divorce. I didn't want it, NOOOOOO!

What actually happened was worse than anything I might have imagined. Victor died, at home one night, from an overdose of sleeping pills. The circumstances were such that I felt responsible; I thought I had killed him.

He had been out late, drinking with a friend. When he returned, waking my mother, they quarreled. Even with my bedroom door shut, I could hear the rise and fall of their voices, in a litany of accusation and blame. Eventually, my mother stormed out of their room, slamming the door behind her. This scenario was familiar to me. If my mother was sufficiently annoyed, she would sleep in the guest bedroom across the hall. I went back to sleep.

Sometime later, I woke to a sound of labored breathing— rasping, gravelly, and hoarse. There was something not right about this sound. It wasn't like snoring exactly; it was slow and gurgly, as if someone were trying to breathe through water. I knew instinctively that it was Victor. His breathing had such a strangled sound that I pictured him choking—on something really scary, like blood. What could, or should, I do about this? What if I was wrong? Everything seemed too unreal in these still, dark, early morning hours for me to act. I lay paralyzed with fear and anxiety, until, once again, I dozed off.

Waking to a cool summer morning, I felt sure that nothing was awry. My night terrors had passed. When I came down to breakfast and found my mother calmly reading the morning paper, I felt doubly relieved. There was nothing out of the ordinary here. Except for the fact that Victor, who sometimes slept late on weekends, had not made an appearance. After a while, my mother went to wake him. When I heard her scream, my nightmare returned.

"He's dead," she cried, rushing down the stairs. "Go look at him," she insisted. "You go look."

I moved to do as my mother asked. But I already knew what I would find.

Ada, though injured, does not die, and even Flora recovers from her anguish over her mother's bloody ordeal. By the end of the film, a new family has evolved, one that is no longer focused on the mother-daughter relationship, with the husband or lover pushed to the margin. As a sign of her acceptance of her mother's alteration, Flora is shown turning cartwheels, an image reminiscent of her carefree dancing to Ada's piano playing on the beach. Surprisingly, everyone in this brooding drama of love and betrayal survives. The atmosphere is correspondingly light—as if a storm had passed, leaving the air fresh and clear.

By tattling on her mother, Flora has set in motion a course of events that changes her world. In her passionate desire to preserve the exclusivity of her relationship with her mother, she hastens its end. Yet Flora's childish act of treason is necessary. Neither Flora nor her mother lives in the fairy-tale realm evoked by Ada's bedtime story of the woman who refuses to be wooed by the wind. The closed circle they inhabit at the beginning of the film is one from which they both need release.

Flora wants her mother as much as she wants and needs to grow up. The intensity of this conflict is reflected in the equally strong passions of her mother. While I saw myself clearly in Flora, I could also see myself in Ada, the strength of whose desire intrigued and frightened me.

Ada's will first causes her to silence herself, for reasons even she does not understand. She "speaks" in her true voice only through her highly colored and idiosyncratic piano playing—until the intrusion of Baines. Succumbing to the force of his erotic interest, she follows a new trajectory until Stewart squarely blocks this path. In the aftermath of her mutilation, she communicates her intent directly to Stewart's mind. "She has spoken to me," as he later explains to Baines. "I heard her voice. There was no sound, but I heard it here," he says, pointing to his forehead. Ada's message concerns the peculiar force of her will. "I have to go, let me go," she says. "I am frightened of my will, of what it might do, it is so strange and strong."

Ada is driven, first by a desire to withdraw from the world of ordinary social interaction, then to surrender to her passion for Baines, who crosses the threshold of her private universe by listening to her play the piano. Entrance into the wordless world of Ada's emotions is perhaps the only avenue to her heart, not to mention the seat of her highly charged eroticism. Only a lover who can hear Ada's thoughts and feelings as expressed in her music has any chance of arousing her from her state of furious self-containment.

The bargain that begins in crass, voyeuristic terms—a key for a peek—slowly evolves into a more complex and unstable interaction. As Baines tires of his position as hungry onlooker, seeking ever more intimate contact, Ada begins to respond to the explicit expression of his desire. His full frontal nudity surprises and disturbs Ada as much as it does the viewer.

Baines's unabashed nudity gives both Ada and us, now in the uncomfortable position of voyeur, a jolt. When he curtails the piano lessons, Ada, in a sudden turnaround, goes to his cabin of her own volition. Frustrated by his lack of comprehension of her intent, she slaps him, beating at his body with her fists. The intensity of her response arouses Baines, who kisses her with equal intensity, igniting Ada's passion. As the lovers begin urgently to undress, the camera focus shifts to the suspicious Stewart, who has followed Ada and now finds himself as mesmerized as Flora by the tantalizing glimpse of the lovers offered by the knothole in the wall. Instead of bursting in to interrupt, he stays to watch.

To what extent was I a voyeur of my mother's relationship with my stepfather, I wonder? In the new house to which we moved shortly after their marriage, my bedroom was adjacent to theirs. Although the walls of the house were thick, I could hear them argue in the middle of the night. I could also hear Victor's death rattle. Did I ever hear them making love? What kind of sex life did they have?

I have reason to believe that all was not well on this score. A longtime friend of my mother's has told me, in somewhat veiled terms, that my mother's honeymoon with Victor was a disappointment. She hinted that my stepfather had a problem. She even speculated that he might have been gay. Because so little was spoken directly, even among the closest of women friends in my mother's circle, it is hard for me to assess this information. Once, in front of me and my two brothers, my mother accused Victor of "cheating" on her. My guess is that she thought he preferred other women, rather than other men. What I knew at the time was next to nothing.

Yet the very fact that my stepfather died in his own bed, after quarreling with my mother, is etched with laserlike clarity on my imagination. Whatever pleasures Victor and my mother may have shared in that bed is a matter of question, but there is no ambiguity about his death.

For many years I was so perturbed by the strength of my wishes and appetites that I suppressed them. It wasn't just that some angry thought I had might actually come to pass, but that I might unwittingly bring harm to someone I loved. It wasn't only the power of hate that alarmed me. I was equally terrified of desire.

For Ada, eros and violence are so closely linked that she pleads with Stewart to release her. The will that once commanded her to be silent now drives her to satisfy her passion for Baines. The urge to communicate with him is so strong that it causes her to despoil her piano of one of its keys. Even the Maoris, who are generally mystified by the ways of the Scottish colonials, understand the meaning of this gesture. The piano "has lost its voice," they say.

There's an obvious parallel between the piano key and Ada's index finger. Both are essential to the emotional fusion with her music that Ada seeks in her playing. When she removes the key from her instrument, she betrays this allegiance, just as Flora betrays her bond with her mother by siding with Stewart. The news of Baines's imminent departure leads to Ada's mutilation of her piano, a decision whose gravity we comprehend long before we witness its bloody consequence. Yet winning her freedom from Stewart does not win her release from her ambivalence. Her will drives her to commit one more impulsive act before she makes peace with her choice to open her life to Baines.

As a canoe carries them away from the shore, Ada signals frantically that she wants her piano dumped into the sea. "She says throw it overboard," Flora translates. "She doesn't want it. She says it's spoiled." The Maori oarsmen, who consider the instrument a death trap, side with Ada against Baines, who tries to dissuade her, fearing that she will regret such a drastic decision. Reluctantly, he helps to maneuver the unwieldy object to the side of the boat. As it topples overboard, Ada steps into the loosened coil of rope at her feet, which tightens around her ankle and yanks her into the water.

Watching this scene for the first time, I didn't know what to think. Does Ada want to kill herself, I wondered, or is she merely acting on a whim? Her lightning response seems on a par with her other decisions, both impulsive and inevitable. In this case, her wordless choice seems to enact her conviction that she, like her piano, is spoiled. Why not follow it to its grave? Ada's body, tethered to her piano, sinking into the ocean literalizes her attachment to silence—her breath escaping in luminous bubbles from her mouth a reminder of her father's prediction that the day she takes it into her head to stop breathing will be her last. Ada's will seems to ordain her death. Is she punishing herself?

I don't remember feeling much in the aftermath of my stepfather's death. I moved around the house in a daze, as people came and went—the family doctor, Victor's law partners, the undertaker. Sometime in the afternoon, while my mother was away making funeral arrangements, I thought to change the sheets on her bed, as if, by an act of housekeeping, to return us to normal, to remove the evidence of violence in our midst. Besides, I couldn't imagine anyone wanting to sleep on the same sheets as a corpse. The only other memory I have from this day is cutting my hand with a kitchen knife as I was slicing ham for sandwiches.

My mother had asked me to make lunch for my two brothers and myself. As I stood steadying the ham hock with my left hand, I noticed that I was aiming the knife in my right hand toward the vulnerable space between my thumb and forefinger. Mentally, I took warning, then calmly watched the blade slide into my flesh, neatly penetrating the surface layers down to the exposed tendon. I had no more reaction to this event than I had to my stepfather's death. It seemed necessary, even inevitable.

"Oh dear," I said, as the blood began welling out of my wound. I walked over to the sink, where my older brother was doing dishes. "Look what I've done," I said. "I've cut myself."

Although my injury was messy, it wasn't dangerous. My brother washed it under the tap, applied an antiseptic, and closed the thin flaps of skin with a butterfly bandage.

If I had had trouble liking my stepfather before his death, I was now indifferent to his fate. Not being able to feel for him, I found it equally hard to feel for myself. My hand with its precise mark of incision was as alien to me as Victor's dead body, as pale and waxy as lard, lying inert in his bed. The only thing I learned from the awful circumstance of his death was how to numb myself. At the same time, I felt that my failure to care made me some kind of monster, someone who deserved to be punished. For many years afterward, the resurgence of any strong emotion would send me into a panic. I didn't know where it might lead, what terrible end might result. I understood Ada's impulse toward self-destruction. Not knowing what harm she might induce in others, she chose to harm herself instead.

If *The Piano* were to rest here—with Ada's willful act of stepping into the noose of rope at her feet—the film would make sense, but it would also be conventional, in the tradition of the nineteenth-century novels it evokes, which call for the transgressive heroine's death. Instead, Campion rescues Ada in mid-drowning. Shoving off her shoe, Ada fights her way to the surface of the water, where, pale and exhausted by this eleventh-hour effort, she gulps in the fresh air. Returning to life and breath, Ada breaks her film-long silence and "speaks" to us directly for a second time in voice-over. "What a death!" she exclaims. "What a chance! What a surprise! My will has chosen life!"

I have never particularly liked the word "will," which I associate with aggressive traits, like power and control—or lackluster ones like persistence or dogged determination. If you will yourself to do something, you force yourself, don't you? I used to think of using my will to perform some distasteful task, like scrubbing the kitchen floor or paying the bills. At worst, I imagined will as something mean, headstrong, or perverse. It never occurred to me that will might also be an active force, a matter of choice, propelled by wish or desire.

For Shakespeare, "will" embraced a wide range of volition, including sexual desire. In his late sonnets, where he writes about lust for a "dark lady," he played with these layers of meaning, while punning on his own name. Ada seems to understand her will in the same spirit. It is the driving force in her life, a kind of primal energy that shapes her actions in ways that interest and upset her. "It has me spooked," she says, "and many others besides."

Ada may be afraid of her will, but she also respects its power. As a teenager, I was merely afraid. It was better not to want anything, I felt, than to want something that might hurt me or someone else. I tried to fit my desires into those of the adults around me. As long as I could please myself by pleasing one of them, I felt satisfied. When I couldn't, I was in a quandary. I wasn't capable of open rebellion. Later in life, when my will impelled me in directions that felt scary to me, I tended, like Ada, to inflict some form of self-punishment. More often than not, this punishment was physical. My body suffered what my soul could not endure.

But wanting is basic, isn't it? How can we do without it? If a baby does not want nourishment, it will starve. If it does not want affection, it will not learn any of the wonders of touch. We come into the world wanting. If thwarted in this primal urge, we lose hope; we dwindle and die. Something within us impels us, long before the development of language or conscious thought, toward life.

Freud, late in his career, struggled to find words for such a powerful force, which strives for human connection even in the face of death. He labeled this messy, inordinate, chaotic bundle of desires "Eros." Set against such an urgent, but unpredictable source of energy, he posited a darker and more solitary impulse, which seeks not to be bothered, to be at rest in an amoebic, undifferentiated state. He called this Darth Vader-like, black-hole mentality, the "death instinct."

For Ada, the "death instinct" represents a condition of perfect fusion, where there is no need for any of the more awkward means of communication like language, because thought and feeling are so fully and flawlessly transmitted. She engages this way with her piano—as if it were a person to whom she is speaking.

But the piano's loss of a key and Ada's loss of a finger spoil such a possibility of fusion. Her connection is severed—literally. It is her choice of a more human and imperfect relationship that ruins her private idyll. Faced with this new and complex reality, she at first rejects it. Only death offers the permanence or purity of silence that she seeks.

In the end, Ada consigns her death wish to the realm of fantasy, to the oddly soothing lullaby of silence she imagines just before sleep, as she pictures her piano in its ocean grave and herself floating above it. Her final voice-over, a quotation from a sonnet by the eighteenth-century poet Thomas Hood, describes the state of being she has renounced. "There is a silence where hath been no sound,/ There is a silence where no sound may be,/ In the cold grave—under the deep, deep sea."

Something nameless in Ada causes her to fight her way back to life. In making this choice, she embraces her own disfigurement, along with the imperfection of her voice as she relearns how to speak. Yet, with the metal fingertip fashioned for her by Baines, which enables her to offer piano lessons, she finds a new identity as the "town freak, which satisfies." Ada's will chooses Eros.

I don't like it when things go badly in the movies. It isn't that I can't tolerate an unhappy ending so much as that I hate the feeling of sick apprehension that comes over me when I am forced to witness a downward turn of events. I had such a feeling of dread when I first watched Ada step into the coil of rope at her feet. "I know where this is heading," I thought, "and I don't want to watch." So I was both surprised and pleased when things took another course. I didn't care about the loss of the piano—or even Ada's finger. I already knew that no one survives into midlife intact. I wanted Ada to live.

I had a feeling of suspension about my own life—as though I were holding my breath somehow, waiting. I associated this feeling with the underwater quality of *The Piano,* an effect that Campion consciously sought. As Stuart Dryburgh, the director of photography explains, "'Bottom of the fish tank' was the description we used to help ourselves to help define what we were looking for. So we played it murky blue-green and let the skin tones sit down in amongst it." Everything in the film leads to the scene of Ada's drowning. It's as though she doesn't really breathe until she breaks through to the surface of the ocean, gasping for air.

The winter of 1994 in Minnesota, where I saw *The Piano* again, felt like a time of suspended animation. Outwardly busy with teaching and administrative work, I was inwardly quiescent. When I went to the movies, more often than not, I found myself crying. Although the ground was frozen under several feet of snow, I felt myself melting or thawing within. It was as though some vast interior ice field were beginning to dissolve. At times I felt flooded, at times overwhelmed. The very act of weeping, instead of lowering my water table of tears, seemed to add to its store. This crying was not convulsive; it was insistent, but also gentle. Water flowed out of me, as if I were some kind of fountain or perpetual spring. I felt like one of those statues of the Madonna that mourn the world's misery through a continuous stream of salt tears.

And then, one day, I began to feel better. The snows gradually shrank, and a wan sun returned, along with the soft, soaking rains of spring. I began to feel sexy and flirtatious, even raunchy. Was all my crying linked to this sudden upsurge of energy? I couldn't stop thinking about the double ending of *The Piano*, which allows Ada to suspend her impulse toward death in favor of the fullness of her passion for Baines. She needs both kinds of awareness, I thought. Her will moves her in both directions, each of which is scary.

The image of Ada floating serenely above her piano anchored to the ocean floor was especially compelling. When I think of my father, who drowned in the Mississippi, I don't picture his body in the graveyard where he is interred. Rather, I imagine him endlessly adrift in the river. For that is where I left him. I understand, as well as Freud or anyone, the seductiveness of death. It isn't only a matter of expiation or self-punishment; it's also a way of bridging our separation from the dead. The call of life, while equally compelling, is full of uncertainty and peril.

Shattering:

Fearless

I was at odds with myself and fragmenting myself.

— St. Augustine, *Confessions*

IN THE AUTUMN OF 1993, I fell and fractured my arm—a hairline crack that did not seem all that significant at the time, but which later struck me as almost pure metaphor. The fracture of my arm was the outward and visible sign of a deeper fissure within, which no mere X ray could reveal. When at last it made its presence felt, the order of my life came apart with a fury that felt to me like Greek tragedy.

I walked into this fateful moment almost literally blind, wearing neither glasses nor contact lenses, as I set out from my house en route to the market a few blocks away. It was a pretty, warmish October day, one of those days when you can enjoy the hot color of the leaves and the late-blooming flowers, when you are happy not to be facing the full force of winter—when it doesn't seem all that important to pay attention to where you are going.

Turning my head at the split-second wrong moment, I toppled off the curb, like a tree ripe for the timber saw. I stepped into air, missed the smooth asphalt grade, twisted my ankle in the gutter beside it, then slammed facedown onto the street, with only my left arm pushed out to break the fall. The shock of this kept me lying there, feeling foolish as cars passed, with passengers leaning out and asking if I needed help. I accepted the offer of two women, who kindly drove me home in their truck. Once safely in my house, I lay down on the couch, as my arm began to swell ominously. It hurt so much that I didn't want to touch it. I lay there, cradling my elbow with my right arm and rocking myself in a primitive effort at self-calming.

By the time my husband Robert came home, the upper part of my left arm was ballooning and turning dark colors, blue-black mostly, with a greenish undertone. Robert was solicitous, but he didn't think I needed to see a doctor. Never having broken a bone before, I wanted to believe him. So I packed some ice in a kitchen towel and wrapped it around my arm, telling myself that it would no doubt feel better in the morning. I took some aspirin and went to bed.

Not being able to sleep for the pain, I moved to the guest room and waited until morning. Robert, who normally rose at 6:00 A.M., came in to check on me. He stood in the door-way, already dressed and ready to leave for work.

"I couldn't sleep," I said. "I think I may have broken something. I'll call a doctor today and see if I can make an appointment." It didn't occur to me to ask Robert for help.

I didn't have a regular internist at that time, so I called an orthopedic surgeon I had seen once years before, assuming that I could get in to see him sooner than someone I didn't know.

"I'm sorry," his receptionist said. "I'm afraid he's booked until Friday. But you can go to the Emergency Room if you think you need to see someone right away."

"Whenever you can work me in," I said, my need suddenly dissipating. "It's probably nothing." I still wanted to believe that my injury, however lurid in appearance, was not serious, that the swelling would go down, that the pain would subside.

Something *was* broken, of course. The X ray showed a non-displaced fracture of the upper tuberosity, which does not require a cast, but does take the usual six weeks to heal. For this period of time, it is important not to move much, to allow the bone to hibernate, to consider the insult to its integrity, to decide whether or not to reknit itself. I scrutinized this shadowy image of my most hidden reality—my scaffolding, the most enduring part of my fleshy upholstery, the thing around which I am built. I saw the fissure in it. I saw how my pure white bone was stressed, how it had pulled, ever so slightly, apart, how it wanted to be cushioned, coddled, even crooned to, until it would consent to reconstitute itself. Hardly knowing what I meant, I vowed to do this.

In the meantime, I tried not to show how I was hurt. I didn't wear the sling, a Velcro affair that just got in my way and made me look odd. But I was aware of how different I was, how hard it was to hold the steering wheel of a car, how impossible to close the door or roll the window up. Being right-handed, I found that I could disguise these things. Only when I accidentally bumped my arm, still swollen and bruised under my long-sleeved turtlenecks and sweaters, would I involuntarily wince. I thought I was bearing my pain with stoicism, with dignity.

From the moment I heard about *Fearless,* a film by Peter Weir based on a novel by Rafael Yglesias about an airplane crash, I had an inordinate desire to see it. Something about its subject appealed to me in my post-fractured state, yet I did not anticipate the visceral nature of its impact.

Fearless opens in near silence, with a close-up view of corn stalks misted with fog or smoke. Gradually, we become aware of a man carrying a baby in one arm, pushing his way through the thick corn. A boy walks beside him, glancing up at his guide for reassurance. The man looks back, motioning others to follow. As these eerie figures emerge from the corn,

we see a group of men standing on an asphalt roadway lit-
tered with pieces of metal. One makes a sign of the cross.

In this long, six-minute sequence of opening images, Weir
interweaves muted, slow-motion takes of the hero Max Klein
with normal sound and action scenes of the crash site. The
result is unsettling, even spooky. While others are flailing or
frantic, Max seems to float through the chaos that surrounds
him, serenely unmoved. When asked by a rescue worker
whether he was on the plane, he shakes his head, deflecting
the man's concern. "I found this baby," he explains. "I'm
looking for its mother." When he locates her, he walks
calmly away and hails a taxi for the nearest motel. After a
shower, he stands in front of the bathroom mirror, scrutiniz-
ing his naked body, slowly moving his hands from his feet,
up his legs and thighs to his breasts and underarms, as if
to confirm his intactness. "You're not dead," he murmurs, in
quiet amazement.

While it's true that Max is not dead, he is not quite alive
either. The feeling of suspended reality generated by the
opening of the film represents Max's inner state of being, in
which he considers himself to be a "ghost," whom nothing
can harm, who is capable of "disappearing" at any moment.
Challenging his newfound sense of invulnerability, he orders
a bowl of ripe strawberries (to which he is allergic) over
breakfast with an old girlfriend at a café. Deliberately, he
chooses one of the largest berries, takes a bite, and swallows.
"See no reaction," he announces coolly. "No reaction at all."
Later, he walks through whizzing cars on a crowded free-
way, then shouts triumphantly "You want to kill me but
you can't!" In answer to his wife, who has been frantic over
his missing status and wants to know why he didn't get in
touch with her immediately, Max says simply, "I thought I
was dead."

In his fearless state, nothing fazes Max—except the rou-
tine responsibilities and ordinary compromises of daily life.

He resists the efforts of the psychologist Perlman to help him understand his post-traumatic stress reaction and orders him out of his house. "I don't want to tell any lies!" he shouts at the lawyer Brillstein, who tries to counsel him on how to manage his lawsuit against the airline. When confronted with the necessity of fudging the truth in order to assist the widow of his partner Jeff, he rushes out of the attorney's office and up to the roof, where he climbs on a ledge, and balancing precariously, muses "Let it go. I could let it go."

Max's behavior is as suicidal as his manner is imperturbable. If he is careless with his life it is because he believes he has no life to lose. A splintered flashback to the moment of the plane crash reveals that Max fully expected to die on impact. "This is it," he tells himself. "This is the moment of your death." He has no fear because the worst, in his mind, has already happened. When he befriends Carla, a woman who is nearly catatonic with grief over the death of her three-year-old boy, he tells her solemnly that she is "safe" driving with him "because we died already." More than once, he invites her to "disappear" with him, advising her to "remember we're ghosts."

When Max crashes his car at high speed into a brick wall in order to demonstrate to Carla that she could not possibly have saved her baby by holding him in her arms (just as she cannot hold onto the toolbox in her lap), he acts to "save" her from her guilt and despair, but in a way that threatens to annihilate himself. Max is not afraid of death; he seeks it. In the film's jolting flashback sequences, which gradually reconstitute Max's experience of the crash, we come to understand how his life seems irretrievably fractured to him, like the smashed aircraft.

The way I held my fractured arm in the fall of 1993—trying to pretend that nothing was wrong—was the way I was used to holding myself, waiting for some inner healing magically to occur. The truth is, I wanted someone to notice my pain, to comfort and soothe me, to assure me that everything would be all right.

At the end of six weeks, my bone fused, but (as a result of my immobility) my whole shoulder had become stuck. My arm still looked bruised and swollen, but the real problem was that I had lost the easy, liquid movement of ball in socket.

"It's a common enough condition," my orthopedist told me. "We call it frozen shoulder."

I had developed adhesions, he explained, a kind of gristle or scar tissue, where there had once been a smoothly oiled mechanism.

"We could anesthetize you," he offered, "and manipulate your arm so as to break these up, or we could see whether physical therapy helps."

I had a flash image of my arm (like that of a wooden puppet) being forced stiffly over my head, making ominous cracking and popping sounds.

"I'll try physical therapy," I said.

I read a story once about a woman skydiver whose parachute didn't open when it should have, plummeting her to earth, like a bird with its wings folded into itself. She broke everything it was possible to break in her body, yet somehow survived. She healed, was not disabled, and became determined to take up skydiving again. My aims were humbler. I wanted to be able to smooth my hair, to fasten a necklace, to hook my bra from behind. But even such simple things seemed beyond my reach; they were so exquisitely fine-tuned, so excruciatingly painful.

I went for therapy twice a week and did, bit by bit, make progress. But my arm continued to feel lifeless, like something more ornamental than useful. I felt like someone who has had an amputation but whose prosthesis is so natural in appearance that no one can tell the difference. I was developing compensatory moves, ways of not revealing the true extent of my dysfunction, until I happened on a new therapist, someone with a genius in his fingers, someone with something like muscular second sight. This man, whose name was Patrick, felt my shoulder as though he were doing a psychic reading, moving my arm in ways that pushed me to the limit of my tolerance of pain, but which also released me.

I found myself looking forward to these visits. They were oddly, but distinctly, erotic. I relished the way he stood behind me, so close that I could smell his scent—a faint mixture of cologne and sweat. I sat in a chair facing a window, which gave us a silky reflection of ourselves against the soft skyline of spring. I could feel Patrick's thigh pressed against my back.

"Is this OK?" he would whisper, as his fingers probed my resistant and yielding places. "How about this? Do you want me to stop?"

Once, we were both so heated by this work that I thought I felt his whole body straining toward me, including his cock.

I wondered if I were being perverse, hating and dreading, but also desiring, this pain. Wanting it because I felt it as something I had to endure to attain a greater good, the free and simple movement of my arm, but also because I liked the physical closeness I felt with my therapist-torturer. This was something that neither of us would speak, a body conversation. We both understood the nature of our bond—that he would inflict and I would accept this level of suffering. But for what? For the elusive aim of healing? Or for the intimacy we felt with each other?

I once knew a man who liked to be hurt. He was a friend, not a lover. He entrusted me with this secret, making it clear that what he meant was not a spiritual form of masochism, but rather something physical, something sexual. I was in my late twenties and very naïve. No way did I want to hear this. I remember feeling a mixture of pity, shame, and fear. How could he admit to such a thing? I didn't know what to do with this knowledge, or even how to remain his friend. I was afraid of such a private world of suffering—of knowing the ways he had been injured, the ways he had been scarred.

My own scars, at that time, were either concealed or invisible. I had a tiny one on my arm, where my younger brother once sliced me with a pair of scissors. We were children then, only two years apart, and fighting about something—who can say what?—perhaps the mere fact that we were so close in age and rivals for our mother's attention. But he was holding this shiny steel instrument, and at some point in our quarrel we each resorted to threat.

"I'll cut you," he said, pointing his weapon toward me.

"I dare you," I replied, not really believing him and in any case refusing to back down.

He reached out and snipped the skin of my inner arm, in the soft, protected space just below the crease of my elbow. I was so outraged that I began to yowl, running to my mother, who would hear none of it.

"If it's true he did this," she said, in a tone of weariness and exasperation, "you must have done something to deserve it."

I was also scarred from pregnancy and childbirth, my belly inscribed with radial white lines indicating how much my abdomen had had to stretch, like the taut skin of a kettledrum, to contain my big baby, my vulva a little jagged around the edges where I had been slit to facilitate her passage. But I felt these wounds as private. No one could discern, just from looking at me, my full history of hurt.

Some part of me, I felt, had been smashed when my father died, as if my whole world had been plucked out of my hands and deliberately, willfully, dashed to the ground. As if I had been holding a precious sphere, which had splintered into a thousand glittering pieces—a toy replica of the earth, which I had inadvertently dropped. There could be no remedy for a tragedy of this sort.

I felt this way about my arm. I had a piece of splintered bone I carried inside me, like shrapnel buried so deep in my flesh that it was impossible to remove without doing more damage than it was worth, something only I could perceive, as it poked and stabbed me from within. Likewise the bruising and swelling on my arm, which took months to subside, as if my interior wound would never close, as if I couldn't stop bleeding under my skin.

When I fell in love some months later, it wasn't for any of the obvious reasons—not for sex, for the pleasure of something forbidden, or even the excitement of being pursued. It was because I saw in this man a fleeting image of myself whole. This is what I wanted. As much as I have ever wanted anything, so much that I was willing to jeopardize the safety of the little world I had laboriously created for myself with Robert. I thought I had been happy with him—as happy as I knew how to be. Yet my inner injuries hadn't healed, or rather they had left me with adhesions, with so much scar tissue that I had forgotten how it felt to move with simple freedom in the world. Falling in love this time was like being anesthetized and ripping up everything all at once.

But at first it felt dreamlike, exhilarating, as if I were falling in slow motion and might never crash. I felt special, as if I were high on LSD and believed I could do anything. I acted like a gambler on a roll. It was as though I were someone else, someone who could beat all the odds, an invulnerable angel who could walk on air.

In an interview in *Movieline* magazine, Peter Weir describes the reaction of his lead actor Jeff Bridges on viewing the first (and only) test screening of *Fearless*. "After that test screen-ing," he says, "Jeff leaned over to me and said, 'It's like you put acid in the popcorn, man.'" Reviewers of the film seem to agree. They use words like "haunting," "hypnotic," and "al-tered states" to convey the film's eerie, quasi-mystical effect. Nearly all comment on Max's weird serenity. "Max is an angel, a saint," observes one. "Maybe he's Jesus, walking on the waters of disaster."

Max's wife Laura objects to Carla's description of him as her personal angel sent to rescue her from despair. "Max is not an angel," she says categorically. "He's a man. He won't survive up there." Laura wants a down-to-earth husband, not an ethereal being who has no regard for the welfare of his family or even the continuation of his own life.

Laura understands her husband's intent when she hap-pens on a portfolio of drawings in his study that appear to represent his experience of the accident. They begin with images of chaotic whirling, like that of a tornado, gradually shading into more formal prints, each of which has a clearly defined black hole at the center. Slowly these drawings give way to ones with a focus on bright light instead of darkness. The last image in this sequence is a reproduction of Hieronymus Bosch's painting *Ascent into the Empyrean,* in which wraithlike figures approach a tunnel that opens into a space of intense illumination. The caption to this painting reads: "The soul comes to the end of its long journey and, naked and alone, draws near to the sun."

Max's fearlessness and seeming invulnerability do not make him an "angel," but someone who is arrested in an am-biguous state between life and death. His last attempt on his life, precipitated by his third deliberate bite of strawberry, unleashes the full flashback memory of the plane crash. This final, eight-minute sequence, most of which takes place in slow motion, to the accompaniment of the haunting first movement of Henryk Górecki's Third Symphony, allows Max's death-trauma to unfold to the point where he must make the choice he has contemplated throughout the film—whether or not to let go.

The extraordinary impact of the replay of the crash is due, not simply to its apparent realism, but to the effect of contrast between the sonorous and slow-building first movement of Górecki's symphony and the fragmentation of the film imagery. Both are intensified by the lack of other sound effects. A look between Max and his wife, who has fetched champagne glasses for the celebration with their lawyer, triggers Max's final, uninterrupted flashback. As he lifts the strawberry to his mouth for a second bite, his wife shouts, "No Max!" and rushes toward him. Max, who has previously shown no reaction to the forbidden strawberries, now falls to the floor in anaphylactic shock.

As viewers, we relive with Max the experience he has hitherto suppressed. "This is it. This is the moment of my death," he muses silently to himself. He then floats through the cabin, reassuring the other passengers, finally taking a seat next to Byron, whom he instructs to lay his head down. "Everything's OK," he says. "It'll all be over soon. Everything's wonderful."

As the plane crash-lands into the cornfield, things begin to fly apart. Pieces of the plane rip away, creating gaping holes in the cabin. A fireball sweeps through, as seats with passengers strapped into them are pulled from their moorings and ejected into the void. Everything devolves into a circular, whirling motion, in which hands, faces, and bodies are mingled and dispersed, like body parts in a giant Waring blender.

At this point I started to cry. I was taken as unawares as I had been over twenty years ago in watching *Pather Panchali*.

I could feel waves of grief surge up from my abdomen, through my chest and esophagus, flowing out of my eyes, my nose, my mouth—convulsing my whole body. I was as helpless as I was embarrassed, squeezing Robert's arm and hiding my face against his sweatered shoulder. Like a kid at a horror movie, I closed my eyes tight, unable to watch what was happening.

"So this is what it's like to die," I thought, echoing Max. "This is how my father felt when he knew he was drowning." Another, more terrifying, thought flashed through me. "I wanted to go with him."

This awareness shocked me. What if, like Sally in *House of Cards,* I wanted to die in order to rejoin my father? How could I go on with my own life? Who would sustain me?

I was too upset to voice such a thought—not even to my husband, who sat beside me, a witness to my breakdown. Having no suspicion of what I was feeling, he didn't attribute any special meaning to this episode.

"I was used to your crying at the movies," he said, some time later, when I asked him what he had made of my reaction. "I didn't make a big deal of it."

I am inclined to think that my body knows everything there is to know about me, the problem being that it is largely mute, a larger problem being that some part of me does not know how to listen.

The other day I read something I consider truly astonishing about the way my body works. It seems that there is a cranial nerve that descends from the base of the brain, like all the others, but which does not flow smoothly down the spinal column. Rather, it wanders. It is indefinite, undecided— vague, vagrant, a vagabond. Hence its Latin designation as the "vagus" nerve. This nerve supplies both motor and sensory impulses to the ear, the pharynx, the thoracic and abdominal viscera, and is involved in such essential functions as swallowing, coughing, and vomiting. It may even provide an alternate route to orgasm. I read this as a sign of the body's deep canniness, its way of tricking us and taking us off guard, as well as its true desire to communicate.

The most secret pathways of our emotions, I believe, are visceral. They travel along the routes forged by the autonomic nervous system, making use of such everyday functions as breathing, digesting, and excreting. Why should it surprise me that my body's most convulsive physical states can give expression to feelings I have wished to deny? More importantly, why have I experienced this condition as a form of captivity or humiliation—an occasion not of relief, but of shame?

In the fall of 1993, I was still baffled by my body's manner of expression. Its vocabulary was nearly as indecipherable as it had been in the winter of 1969 when I first viewed *Pather Panchali*.

No doubt I was upset by breaking down in such a public place as a movie theater while watching *Fearless,* but my distress exceeded that of mere embarrassment or exposure. As the airplane began to disintegrate, I felt as though something inside me was flying apart. It felt like experiencing my father's death, while knowing that I would survive him. I had another image for this awareness. It was like having my skin torn off.

Max's full traumatic flashback triggered my own. For a moment, I was completely open to this experience—in a way I could not have allowed myself to be as a child. Had I not gone into something like shock at that time, I do not know whether I would have had the simple, dogged will to live. Sometimes not feeling or not knowing the extent of one's injuries is a blessing. When it's best not to look in the mirror.

But there is also a time for acknowledging the truth of one's alteration—and a time to mourn that loss.

Sitting in the movie theater, watching *Fearless,* I was unable to reflect on my reaction. Instead, I literally closed my eyes. In my need to avoid Max's final flashback memories of the plane's disintegration, I missed the frames that precede his gasping return to life—much as I had "forgotten" the movement toward reconciliation at the end of *Solaris.* At this point in time, I could not imagine anything other than a tragic conclusion.

Yet the film continues—alternating between shots of Max rising from the wreckage of the downed plane and lying on his living-room floor, while his wife frantically administers mouth-to-mouth resuscitation. In a long shot, we view Max walking toward a source of brilliant illumination at the end of the sheared-off cabin. With calm precision, he takes the hand of Byron and, turning back to the other survivors, mouths the words, "Follow me to the light." In the meantime, sensing that he is slipping away from her, his wife (in between breaths) shouts, "No Max!" Next, we see Max alone in the empty shell of the plane cabin, gazing backward over his shoulder before turning toward the streaming light. Max is on the point of completing the journey he anticipated from the first warning signals of the disaster when he lurches back into the present—choking, then laughing, and hugging his wife. "I'm alive," he exclaims, in amazement, "I'm alive."

Max's drawings express not only his conviction that he will die, but also his attraction to this prospect. In his mind, death is not something to fear, but a goal as clear and inexorable as the light that beckons him from the end of the plane cabin. Nothing in his actual, everyday life seems as real—hence his uncompromising stance with the lawyer, along with his conviction that he is a ghost. What makes him turn back? What makes him choose life?

When Max meets Carla, she is so despondent over the death of her son that she refuses to leave her darkened bedroom. "Let me die," she pleads with her husband Manny, "I want to die." Instead of trying to rouse her from her lethargy, Max starts talking about his father's death when he was a teenager. "My father died when I was thirteen," he says, describing in detail the scene of his father's fatal heart attack.

"That was God," Carla replies.

"That's what I thought. God killed my dad."

"Why would he want to do that?" Carla asks, suddenly interested.

"Couldn't figure that out," Max answers candidly. " So I decided there's no God."

While Carla is God-obsessed, believing that she will be punished for lying to her lawyer and to her confessor about how she held onto her son Bubble at the moment of the plane's impact, Max is serenely agnostic. "If life and death just happen," he points out, "there's no reason to do anything." "No reason to love," Carla replies, exposing the flaw in Max's logic. Carla resists Max's characterization of her as a phantom, finally telling him in no uncertain terms that she is "not a ghost anymore," and that she wants him to go home. "I want you to live again," she says. "You can't save everybody. You have to take care of yourself."

When Max returns home from the hospital where he is treated for his automobile-crash injuries, he first apologizes to his son Jonah for an angry outburst, then leafs through the scrapbook Jonah has assembled containing the newspaper accounts of his heroism. Pausing over the cutout words "Bravery Saves Passengers," Max appears to reflect on Carla's advice. On entering the kitchen, he announces to Laura, "I want you to save me."

In the fall of 1993, I too was looking for someone to save me. I was looking for someone who promised more than the kind of healing I received from my physical therapist. I wanted someone who could integrate my psyche. When I fell in love some months later, the stakes were high. I wasn't looking for romance; I was looking for salvation.

My lover attracted my attention in the simplest of possible ways—by listening to me. I hadn't been aware, until this moment, of how starved I was for conversation, in particular for someone with whom I could talk about my inner life. As I began to unfold the stories I had held so tightly wound up inside me, I experienced a curious light-headedness, which gradually expanded into euphoria. I felt simultaneously giddy and safe—as if I were walking a tightrope strung over an abyss, with ease and surefootedness. It was this feeling that held me spellbound. Some part of me knew that I was courting disaster, but I couldn't stop.

I felt at peace with myself in my lover's embrace. He encouraged me, praised me, soothed me, and reflected me back to myself in a way I had never experienced. In the mirror of his regard, I felt singular and intact—as though all the scattered pieces of myself, as in time-lapse photography, were slowly assembling themselves into a coherent whole. It was as if the fractured continental plates of the earth were to heal their ancient rifts, drifting back into a single landmass. This is how I wanted to see myself—like a NASA satellite looking down on the beautiful little sphere of the earth—viewing myself as something so precious that no one could possibly want to hurt it.

When my lover offered to do things for me, saying he was

willing to perform any task, I felt like a fairy-tale princess invited to voice her heart's desire in the form of a wish. I asked him to repair a small, painted wood figure of an angel I had bought in a Mexican gift shop the year before, which had fallen from my living-room mantel and cracked in two. "Just glue her back together," I said. "She doesn't need to be perfect."

My lover, intuiting the significance of this assignment, took it to heart. He spent several days reattaching the angel's severed parts, carefully filling in the chips and gaps, then more weeks cruising art-supply stores for the exact shade of blue to match the color of her gown. The result was everything I could have hoped. "She's seamless," I said, "even I can't see the break."

I thought about Henry James's novel *The Golden Bowl,* in which the barely detectable flaw in an exquisitely crafted piece of crystal comes to stand for the fissure in the central characters' marriage. While I was in search of some image of perfect inner healing, which I associated with my lover's tender care of me, my own marriage cracked open, splitting irrevocably apart. Since then, I have lost the free-fall sense of invulnerability I experienced in the beginning of my affair. Like Max, waking from his dreamlike, post-crash state, I am no longer fearless.

St. Augustine was in his early forties when he wrote his *Confessions.* I was in my mid-fifties when I read it for the first time. When I came to the pivotal chapter eight, which describes the moment of his conversion, I was struck not so much by the suddenness (or even the spiritual nature) of this change as by the inner struggle and anguish that precede it. All of the conflicts of Augustine's life seem concentrated in the space of a single afternoon. He comes to a house with friends, where his whole life passes before him, over-whelming him with self-loathing and disgust. In a state of "violent conflict," he separates himself from his compan-ions, and enters a small garden, where he tears his hair and batters his forehead, feeling that he may be going mad. "I was at odds with myself and fragmenting myself," he says. Finally, he gives in to his distress. "A huge storm blew up within me and brought on a heavy rain of tears," he tells us. "I flung myself down somehow under a fig tree and gave free rein to the tears that burst from my eyes like rivers." This is like my convulsive crying, I thought. He's having a nervous breakdown.

In the "intense bitterness of [his] broken heart," some-thing unexpected happens. Suddenly, Augustine hears an unearthly voice singing from somewhere nearby. "Pick it up and read," it calls to him. As if on cue, he stops crying and follows the voice's command—as if it were a divine sum-mons. In this quasi-hypnotic state, he picks up the Bible and reads the following: "Go and sell all you possess and give the money to the poor; you will have treasure in heaven. Then come, follow me." As if by magic, Augustine knows what to do with his life. He feels the excruciating pain of his inner conflict resolved.

When I saw *Fearless*, I felt no inner resolution of conflict. Rather, I was just beginning to enter into the field of disinte-gration that I associated imagistically with the plane crash. Crying in the spasmodic way that I did was only the first stage in my private process of conversion. I felt at first (and at length) as if I were having some kind of nervous breakdown, at odds with myself and, like St. Augustine, sobbing out the bitterness of my broken heart. This phase, which coincided with the most physically excruciating stages of healing for my frozen shoulder, blended seamlessly into the beginning of my affair, which offered a brief, though memorable, respite from my sense of inner fragmentation.

I wonder sometimes how we come into the world—perfect or fallen? Or perhaps neither, maybe just disassembled. The French psychoanalyst Jacques Lacan would say that we cannot perceive ourselves whole until we receive a mirror reflection of ourselves—in the gaze of our mother or some other caring adult. The kind of image I wished for, perhaps, in my lover's adoring regard. Such a reflection, Lacan would say, is what allows us to grasp the idea of our integrity. But such a notion of coherence is an illusion, a will-o'-the-wisp that we are constantly recreating or seeking after.

When my daughter Jessica was born, I remember thinking she looked wise. I have a picture of her, taken by her father, that captures this awareness for me. She is lying in her crib, with only a diaper on, one arm slung loosely around her fuzzy bear, the other raised as if to signal something—like those paintings of the Christ child with a tiny globe in one hand, the other lifted in greeting.

But I was no Virgin Mary. In order to make my daughter I had had to break, my whole body in some kind of crisis of expansion and expulsion. What had been planted inside me as the least discernible, most fragile form of life could only come to fruition through a fracture of my own, through a breach such as I had never imagined.

I once tried to say this in a poem:

> Before she broke my still, hard womb
> In the clear glass I saw myself
> Naked and firm as unripe fruit.
> But, wrenched by that ungainly act,
> My image is obscured by blood.
> I can't remember what I knew.

Now my birth-changed body seeks
What it can only contemplate:
The wisdom of her final form
Her ghostly head and childish bones.

Perhaps the wisdom, the wholeness, the sense of healing or resolution that we spend our lives seeking is similarly ghostly. Not unreal, but elusive, like a dream of happiness we forget on waking, leaving its perfume, but evaporating and receding before us—just beyond our grasp.

Transgression:

The Cement Garden

> Say that we had one father, say one womb
> (Curse to my joys) gave us both life and birth;
> Are we not therefore to each other bound
> So much the more by nature, by the links
> Of blood, of reason—nay, if you will have't,
> Even of religion—to be ever one,
> One soul, one flesh, one love, one heart, one all?
>
> — John Ford, *'Tis Pity She's a Whore* (1633)

THE ONLY TIME I TRIED to talk with my mother about my father's death, she became so upset with me that I had to apologize.

"You're giving me nightmares," she said. "Go home. I want you to leave." She was shaking as she glared at me from across the kitchen. But her voice was hard, insistent.

I walked over to her and put my arms around her. "I'm sorry," I murmured, "I'm so sorry." If I left then, I didn't know how I could ever come back.

"Promise me you'll never talk about this again. You have to promise."

"All right," I said, "I promise."

The subject of my father's death was taboo, literally unspeakable. My older brother was the only one who would talk to me, my sole confidant. Only he seemed to share my sense of loyalty to Dad's memory. Yet he was also seductive. Over time, our childhood sex play opened the door to a more powerful temptation, one that felt even more unspeakable than death. Most of my life, I have avoided thinking about it. Yet the things I most want to suppress from my awareness tend to be the ones that develop the most flourishing and intractable life of their own—the ones that drive me to act in unpredictable ways.

In the summer of 1994 when I first saw *The Cement Garden,* a film by Andrew Birkin based on the novel by Ian McEwan, I was in the midst of the affair that led to the breakup of my second marriage. I saw this film with my lover, thinking it might help me to understand what I was doing. I was drawn to this man with irresistible force. His presence was a charged field, reminding me of my one experience of a MRI, a medical imaging process that reveals the intimate structure of your soft tissues. When I told him this, searching for words to express how I felt with him, he said simply, "I'm inside you."

But what did this mean? Did I even want him there? Having someone penetrate that deeply into my interior frightened me. What would he find? A crypt? A carrion mess? Or something flourishing and full of life? How, also, could I permit such an intrusion? Wasn't any kind of sex in these circumstances wrong? How could I consent to betray my husband?

I found myself wanting to do everything my lover suggested, wishing to offer myself in every way possible to his desire, at the same time that I felt a terrible condemnation for these impulses. What did this say about me? Was I some kind of call girl or high-class whore? I didn't know how to deal with these reactions. But I sensed that *The Cement Garden,* an offbeat tale of brother-sister incest, had something to tell me about my own history, something urgent that I needed to attend to.

In *The Cement Garden* there is an inevitability to the course of events that portrays the movement toward sibling incest as

somehow fated (hence blameless), as well as profoundly dis-
quieting. First, the father of a working-class British family
dies of a heart attack in the midst of an attempt to cement
over the garden he has laboriously constructed in the back
of his house. It isn't long before the mother, suffering from
some undiagnosed, yet clearly wasting disease follows. The
four siblings, confronted with the possibility that they may
be separated by the authorities and farmed out into foster
homes, band together in suppressing the fact of their mother's
death. The two oldest, the adolescents Julie and Jack, decide
to bury her in the basement, submerging her body in a metal
locker filled with cement. For a while, the children manage
well enough on their own, with Julie suddenly thrust into
the role of Mother, while her slightly younger brother acts
as surrogate Father.

Yet changes take place. Domestic order begins to unravel
as dishes pile up on the kitchen table and in the sink, and
each of the orphaned siblings follows his or her most powerful impulse toward comfort. While Julie revels in her new
position of authority, Jack retreats into a private fantasy
world, made up of equal parts of sci-fi reading and mastur-
bation. Tom, the youngest, who is the most voluble about
missing Mum, is content to be dressed up as a girl by his sisters or to be treated as a baby, put to bed with a bottle in a
crib. Sue, the next in age, assumes the role of observer, keeping a daily journal, addressed to her absent mother, in which
she details the bizarre happenings around her. Though a bit
odd, this family is basically functional—until the appearance
of the outsider Derek, who arrives in a conspicuous red
sports car to court Julie.

Derek not only disturbs the field of erotic tension surrounding Jack and Julie, he also challenges the bond of se-
crecy that isolates and protects the siblings' family unit.
His gift to Julie of a pair of expensive boots clearly annoys
Jack, who shows his resentment by exaggerating his already

slovenly manner and rude behavior. Julie, aware of Jack's obscure longing for her, alternately flirts with him (kissing him on the lips in one scene) and pushes him away, while refusing to let Derek in on the truth about Mother. When Derek inquires about a suspicious smell emanating from the basement, she deflects his question by claiming, "It's probably Jack; he hasn't bathed in weeks." Later, when Derek decides to investigate, she sides with Jack, who offers the unlikely explanation that the smell comes from the remains of a family dog, buried in the (now cracking) cement. In this crucial scene, the four siblings band together against the outsider who threatens their fragile family constellation, supporting Jack's impromptu lie and forcing Derek to depart.

That evening Jack enters his mother's bedroom, sits at her vanity gazing into the mirror, and finally falls asleep, naked on her bed. Wakened by the sound of Tom crying from Julie's room, he goes to comfort him, climbs into his cot, and sings Mother's "Sandman" song to help him sleep. Julie finds them there, curled up together like "two bare babies." Jack climbs out of the cot and wraps a sheet around his waist, as Julie confesses that she has not slept with Derek. She pulls him over to her bed and begins to caress his shoulder, murmuring, "Just you and me and Sue and Tom." She undresses, pushes Jack's hair away from his face and kisses him, then rolls over on top of him.

"I've lost all sense of time," she says.

"It's always been like this," Jack concurs. "Everything seems fixed, still."

Just then, Derek appears in the bedroom doorway. "How long has this been going on?" he challenges.

"Ages, ages," Julie replies dreamily, holding her brother's hand and smiling.

Derek leaves in disgust.

This time, Julie lies back, while Jack kisses her. "Do you think we did the right thing?" she asks.

"Seems natural to me," he replies.

"Me, too."

A dull pounding is heard—from the sound of Derek wielding a sledgehammer against the cement block in the basement—as Jack and Julie begin to make love. The pounding increases in tempo as the lovers' passion reaches its crescendo. The last shot shows the two asleep, while a blue light from a police car in the street shines through the bedroom window, flashing across their naked bodies.

The scene where Julie and Jack make love is simultaneously beautiful and shocking. My reactions were equally conflicted. With one part of myself I felt the naturalness of Jack and Julie's responses to each other, while with another I felt like Derek, who calls in the police to expose their transgression. This scene was so disturbing to me that it sent me on a mental journey through my own sexual history. When and how did I learn that sex is wrong or that certain activities are forbidden? More importantly, how was this history affecting me in the present?

I have only two memories of uninhibited expression of sexual curiosity from my early childhood. One involves my best friend Janet, who lived across the street from me and whom I played with daily before we entered kindergarten. I had already learned how to masturbate, though I had no words as such to describe what I was doing or how I felt. One day, when we were both taking a nap in the afternoon at her house, I started touching myself under the covers, describing to her how "it feels good and then better and better until you want to stop." It seemed natural to share this experience with Janet because she was my very best friend. I didn't feel that I was doing anything wrong.

My second memory is more complex.

When I was very young, my mother used to bathe my two brothers and me together on Saturday night. On other days, a quick face-and-hand wash was enough. The full Saturday-night bath was like changing underwear and bed-sheets, a once-a-week occurrence. So powerful was this ritual—at which we also had our ears cleaned and our toe-nails clipped—that for years I thought people who bathed or showered everyday were overly anxious or somehow obsessive.

Our house had one bathroom for five people, yet I don't remember feeling pinched for space, except when I had an urgent need and someone else was occupying the toilet. On the Saturday night in question, my brothers and I were splashing around in the tub, while my mother hovered near, allowing us a moment of play before undertaking the serious business of scrubbing. My father stood at the sink in his undershirt, shaving. Perhaps they were getting ready to go out that night.

I was sitting facing my older brother in the tub, when suddenly I noticed his penis—as if for the first time. Bobbing and floating in the water, it looked curious and interesting.

"Why is that so pink?" I asked, saying the first thing that popped into my mind.

Instantly, the atmosphere in the room changed—like the way that wind dies down or light shifts before the advance of a coming storm.

"That's it!" my father exploded, as invisible hands reached into the tub and whisked me out onto the floor. "This is the last time they take a bath together."

I was used to my father's mercurial changes of temper but had no idea of what I had done to provoke such a dramatic response. Needless to say, my question went unanswered. It hung in the air, acquiring a mystery and gravity I hadn't an-ticipated and could not fathom.

This was the moment at which sex (and sexual difference) acquired meaning for me. No longer a matter of simple exploration, it was suddenly charged with danger and electricity. I felt responsible for this alteration, which also signaled the end of innocence. From this point forward, sex play between me and my two brothers—which was memorable though relatively infrequent—acquired a special kind of excitement. We had entered the zone of the forbidden.

There were two other incidents before my father died.

In the first, I was seven or eight years old and sick in bed. Some playmates (two boys, I think) had come to visit me in order to watch television, since few families in our neighborhood owned one as yet. It was late afternoon, and something like *Howdy Doody* was on. My brothers suggested that we show ourselves to one another. I watched while furtive unzipping and touching went on. Since I was in bed with the covers up, I was an observer, though an increasingly excited one. I was also frightened that we would be discovered and felt relieved when the game ended.

The next morning my dad strode into my room while I was dressing for school and confronted me. One of the neighbor children had confessed, and his parents had called my parents to complain. While I was still taking in this information, my dad slapped me hard across the face and then left. Because I loved him absolutely, I felt pained and humiliated. Although I was used to being reprimanded and even spanked on occasion, I had never before been hit on the face. I could hardly even remember what had happened the day before to provoke such a violent reaction. My mother also made an issue of this incident, asking me later if I had remembered to report my sin to the parish priest at weekly confession. In my first deliberate lie to her, I said yes.

The second incident, which occurred a couple of years later, involved only me and my older brother. We were both sick this time and confined to bed in our separate, but adjoining, rooms. My mother was out grocery shopping. I was bored with reading, my usual pastime, when my brother called me from the next room. He wanted to try something new, he said, something that I might like. Carefully he explained how he wanted to put his penis in my mouth. He didn't actually say "penis," since neither of us was acquainted with this word. Much later, when I encountered it in a sex manual, I pronounced it "pen-is," making it sound like some kind of exotic writing utensil. If I did this for him, he assured me, he would do something similar for me. I agreed.

First, he went to the bathroom to wash himself, then lay back in his bed, while I bent over him, trying to follow his instructions. He was still too young to have a full erection or orgasm, but he seemed satisfied with my efforts. "It's my turn," I said finally, wanting to be sure we had time to switch roles before my mother came back. This time, I washed then lay down, though I insisted that I lie on the floor, in the space between my brothers' twin beds, as if to protect us from prying eyes. I thought that if we were both somewhat hidden from sight that we would not be caught off guard.

While my experiences touching myself had prepared me to feel pleasure, I was awakened to an entirely new range of sensation that languid afternoon. My brother, as if exquisitely attuned to every nerve ending in my vulva, licked me slowly upward. Not only did I have no words for the parts of my body he aroused into such vibrant expression, I had no way to give voice to the intensity of need and desire that I felt. I did, however, know that what we were doing was wrong—that is to say that we would be shamed and punished if we were found out. This double awareness caused me, finally, to tell him to stop. While every fiber in my body wanted to continue, I was also acutely aware of time passing. What if my mother came home just now? What if she discovered us like this? I remembered my father's anger and his hand across my face. This time my transgression was far worse.

As it happened, we escaped detection. I insisted on lowering my nightgown and returning to my own room long before my mother came home. While still aroused, I was also relieved. By this time, I knew that mere exploration of bodily sensation was off-limits—as exciting as it was forbidden.

The Cement Garden shows erotic tension building between Jack and Julie in the aftermath of Father's death. In one scene, Jack enters Julie's room, wearing thick gloves and a large, beehive tender's hat. In mock menace, he approaches Julie, who enters the spirit of the game by pretending to cringe in fear. Wrestling her into bed, Jack begins to tickle her mercilessly. Helpless with laughter, Julie tries to defend herself. Suddenly, a change occurs. Unable to catch her breath, Julie appears to be in real distress. As the film speed slows, we watch her clutch at Jack's body and face with her hands. Her labored breathing, coupled with the look of intensity on her face, mimic the throes of passion. Jack's body, pressed against hers, pushes her short skirt up, exposing her bare thighs and white panties. He gazes down at her crotch, then backs away from her abruptly. "Get out," Julie says to him coldly. "Get . . . out." Both siblings recoil from what appears to be a recognition of mutual desire.

There is one more incident that signals Jack and Julie's awareness of their reciprocal attraction before Mother dies—leaving them with no parental figure either to mitigate or to bar the expression of their erotic impulses.

Because Mother is too weak to get out of bed, Jack's birthday is celebrated in her room, with fresh-squeezed orange juice made by Sue and a cake baked by Julie. Tom cuddles close to his mum, while all sing "Happy Birthday" to Jack. In the awkwardness that ensues, Julie challenges Jack to do something. "Why don't you sing us a song?" she says. When Jack refuses, Sue suggests that Julie perform. Looking straight at Jack, she does a handstand, which causes her skirt to fall down over her head, revealing her slim thighs and white panties. Slowly, she moves her legs apart, emphasizing the exposure of her crotch. Jumping to his feet, Jack begins to sing "Greensleeves" in a wavering falsetto voice, which suddenly breaks and changes register, as if to signal a shift in erotic awareness. At the end of this impromptu scene, Jack stares silently at Julie, who leans toward him and kisses him on the cheek.

In *The Cement Garden,* desire between brother and sister is mutual, but it is the (somewhat older) sister who takes the initiative. In my family, these roles were reversed. Not only was my brother Bob my chief source of information about what adults did with each other sexually, but he was also the one who gave voice to and acted on the current of feeling that ran between us. In my anxiety, I took refuge in taking the more passive and more submissive role. In this way, I could try to persuade myself that it wasn't really my idea and hence was not my fault.

It was Bob who told me, quite bluntly, about intercourse—how a man inserts his "thing" into a woman's body, though I'm not sure he included the information about how babies are made. Still, I was so rattled that I claimed not to believe him. Although I had seen my brother's penis in the bathtub, I had not explored my own body in this way. Where was this hole, this point of entry? I had never looked at myself that carefully and was too confused or ashamed to try. I sensed that my brother was not lying, but was too shocked to want to investigate. I took in what he said, but let it lie fallow, not wanting to disturb the relatively simple order of my understanding up until this moment.

Bob and I were both growing up willy-nilly—without the guidepost of our father, who not only set the rules in our family, but who also provided its center of love. Without him, my mother, two brothers, and I were vulnerable and adrift. We struggled on a daily basis to figure out what to do.

My mother once confessed to me how panicked she felt at this time.

"I had to make all the decisions," she said. "But I had never even written a check before, and you children kept asking me questions about everything."

I held my breath, knowing that if I interrupted her, she would fall silent again. I would lose whatever revelation was in store.

"You even wanted me to tell you which socks to wear in the morning," she continued with exasperation. "It nearly drove me crazy."

In *The Cement Garden,* Julie, Jack, Sue, and Tom each work at keeping the household together after the death of Father. No one discusses the impact or implications of Mother's sickness until Mother herself broaches this subject with Jack. She will be going to the hospital, she tells him, for some tests. "You and Julie will have to be in charge," she says. When Jack demurs, she counters with a threat. "If you don't, they'll come and take Tom and Sue into care. Maybe you, too." Driving home her point about Tom's special need and vulnerability, she insists, "You and Julie have to be like Mum and Dad to him, until I get back."

When Mother dies, Jack and Julie take her instructions literally. They first join hands in the scheme to conceal the fact of her death—deciding not to inform the authorities, who will undoubtedly break up the family—and to bury her themselves. Together, they mix the cement that will encase their mother's body, moving her to the basement where they inter her in a metal locker.

Mixing the cement is like playing with mud. Julie's and Jack's hands touch in this mess as they work feverishly to accomplish their task. At one point, Jack cleans a speck of dirt from Julie's eye. Together, they struggle with the issue of who will move Mother's body from the bed, who will drag it down the stairs. They are accomplices in a crime that neither sees as such—the magnitude of which neither can comprehend. After this deed, they cannot avoid the role of surrogate parents—playing Mum and Dad.

I don't think that my brother and I thought of ourselves as playing house—in the way that children sometimes do in their explorations of each other's bodies. Nor were we literally orphaned, like Julie and Jack. My mother was very much alive, though profoundly distracted, not only by her grief, but also by the everyday demands of keeping our household together. Whatever else happened to us as a family, we were at least not separated. Yet when I first viewed *The Cement Garden* I saw a connection between Julie and Jack's dilemma and my own. While my mother was physically present, caring for me and my two brothers, making sure that we ate, slept, washed, dressed, and went to school on time, she was emotionally removed. Her body was there, but her soul was elsewhere. The lively mother we had once had had vanished as surely as our father. Some part of her seemed to have died with him, leaving my brothers and me alone with our grief.

Once, when we were adults, Bob told me how my mother expected him to step into my father's shoes.

"Suddenly I was the man around the house," he said. "Whenever anything didn't work, I was supposed to fix it."

"What did you do?" I asked. "How did you cope?"

"I was scared," he confided, "but pretended that I wasn't. When the washing machine broke down, I just kept tinkering with it, until somehow I figured out what was wrong."

My brother, at age twelve, had had to grow up fast, assuming the responsibilities of a grown man. At age nine, I was protected from the cares of running a household, but not from the pain of loss. In this respect, Bob and I were on equal ground. Not only did we both miss our dad, we both felt the change in our mother.

In *The Cement Garden,* Julie, Jack, Sue, and Tom, while struggling to maintain some kind of family unity, adapt to their radically altered circumstances in ways that are unique to each. While Julie assumes command of preparing meals in the increasingly messy kitchen and Jack withdraws into his sci-fi fantasy world, Tom plays at being a girl or a baby. Sue stands on the sidelines, retreating to the basement to write in her journal. Each, in his or her own way, is trying to hold onto some vestige of the familiar. By pretending to be an intact family, they are also waging a war against time.

The decision to bury Mum in the basement, though prompted by the fear of separation, acts as a denial that anything has changed. In the world the siblings desperately try to inhabit there is no acknowledgment of the reality of death—only strategies for maintaining the status quo. The visual field of the film also conveys this message. Scenes alternate between the chaotic interior of the family dwelling and a broken-down house in a wasteland of weeds and concrete. Coming on Tom (in a wig and a skirt) with his friend William playing in one of these deserted rooms, Jack asks what they are doing. "He's being Julie," William states, referring to Tom. "Who are you?" Jack inquires. "He's being you," Tom answers. In the midst of ruin, Tom is doing his best to mimic the order that his older siblings are laboring to create at home.

Derek destabilizes this situation through his attentions to Julie and his inquisitiveness, which threatens to expose the family secret. Jack, who is obviously aroused by Julie's proximity, becomes openly jealous in the presence of Derek, who clearly suspects that something is awry in this parent-less household. In the film's turning-point moment, the siblings unite around Jack's lie to expel the intruder. The incest consummated between Jack and Julie seals this bond. Brother and sister are acting not only on mutual attraction but also out of a common aim—to forestall the ravaging effects of change. In this sense, playing Mum and Dad is a way to hold the forces of entropy at bay.

A repeated, dreamlike sequence in the film, which first occurs after Mum's burial, portrays the futility of this attempt. In it, we see a red kite sailing lazily in the sky over a beach, where children busy themselves covering someone's legs and feet with sand. Jack, the dreamer, wakes suddenly—with a hard-on. When this scene recurs, it is no longer attached to Jack's dreaming state, though it appears to represent his inarticulate feelings of loss. This time, we see the red kite flying, while a man, woman, and girl in a green bathing suit walk down the beach, away from the viewer. In one sequence, the woman, wearing a forties'-style dress, glances briefly back. The color symbolism of this scene—the green of the bathing suit alluding to Julie's lime-green bikini, the red to Derek's red sports car—is less clear than the action, which seems to represent the childhood family unit from which Jack is now excluded. Yet, if the green bathing suit points to the object of Jack's desire, the red kite signals the disruptiveness of its expression. If wanting his sister Julie stands in part for Jack's wish to keep things as they are, the act of possessing her destroys that possibility. In the logic of the film, Derek's intervention is as inevitable as Julie and Jack's incest. One calls for the other. In the next-to-last scene, the red kite spirals slowly downward, as if to demonstrate not only the evanescence of Jack's desire but also the fantasy that sustains it.

Although I did not, finally, make love with my older brother, I wanted to. He felt comforting to me, his maleness sufficiently other to be exciting, yet also familiar enough to put me at ease. He was the closest I could get to my beloved—and absent—father. Although our childhood sex play made me anxious, it also stimulated me. Like Julie or Jack in their specially vulnerable, orphan state, I did not know how to resist the welter of longing and desire that I felt. Who, but my brother, could understand what I had been through? Who else could offer me solace?

Seeing *The Cement Garden* with my lover helped me to explore the roots of my attraction to my older brother. It reminded me of another story of sibling incest, John Ford's seventeenth-century play *'Tis Pity She's a Whore,* which had made quite an impact on me when I first encountered it as a graduate student. In it, the protagonist Giovanni describes his sister Annabella as someone so close to him that they are almost Siamese twins. Having shared the same father, the same womb, they are, he says, forever bound, "one soul, one flesh, one love, one heart, one all." Intense romantic or sexual love creates this illusion, I think, but Giovanni tries to force things by choosing someone as like himself as possible in order to satisfy his wish for perfect union. Ford's play, combined with my viewing of *The Cement Garden* gave me another way to understand my incestuous involvement with my brother.

I was in my early twenties, and it was the late sixties—a time when anything having to do with sex was regarded as liberating, if not revolutionary. Even the subject of brother-sister incest seemed approachable, acceptable, or at the very least stageable. Still the costuming for the play, performed by the Yale Drama School, was radical for its day. Both Annabella and her brother Giovanni were dressed in flesh-colored, skin-tight bodysuits, revealing every contour, every suggestive protuberance of their svelte young bodies. This was no inhibited, frustrated, ultimately impossible love. It was frank, open, and seemingly enjoyed by both. Giovanni and Annabella didn't just talk about sex, they acted on their passion.

From the point of view of the protagonists, incest appears to be unproblematic. As in *The Cement Garden,* the lovers do not condemn themselves; nor do they repent. Rather, they die in a state of sin—outrageous and defiant. When Annabella's pregnancy is discovered, Giovanni murders her and carves out her heart, brandishing it publicly on his sword. Although his action calls for retribution, he seems to revel in his crime. Intervention and punishment come from another source.

Watching the play, I was nonplussed. I didn't know where to place myself—with Annabella and Giovanni in the expression of their mutual desire or with the voices raised against them. I took refuge in peripheral concerns. Annabella's heart impaled on her brother's sword looked too big to me. Where did they get this stage prop, I wondered—in a butcher shop? Instead of being impressed with the tragic conclusion of the story, I felt emotionally removed, as if I were witnessing a black comedy or a farce. Yet Ford's play did have relevance to me, not only in terms of my long-ago attraction to my older brother, but also in the love drama unfolding in my present.

I was falling for a fellow graduate student in English, who was the first man (other than my brother) whom I allowed to touch me intimately. We started with kissing—which was a world in itself—and for a long time I was satisfied with this. With exploring the contours of his mouth, feeling the different qualities of softness, hardness, and smoothness of his lips, teeth, and tongue. How wonderfully equal, reciprocal, even genderless this felt. We each had the same equipment, the same complex interior space, the same supple and muscular organ. Kissing was a revelation to me, a little biosphere of pleasure. My brother and I had never kissed.

Gradually, we moved downward, in a leisurely progress toward my breasts. This was the part I most loved—knowing that at some point in our fully clothed embrace his hands would begin to caress my nipples through my blouse. It was easier, I discovered, if I wore something that buttoned in the front. Then his fingers would seek to lift a nipple from my bra. Not disrobing me, but something infinitely more sexy— pushing my still-fastened brassiere down far enough to release my breast. From this point, I was rapt. No matter how many times we repeated this scenario, I never tired of it.

My graduate-school lover—I'll call him "Joe," the name his ditzy alcoholic landlady used, mistaking him for another roomer—seemed as mesmerized as I was by our languorous foreplay. Which might never have moved to a more critical stage, had it not been for an accident that occurred one night at her house.

Jean had been drinking, as she often did alone, in the lower half of her duplex. Usually we ignored her querulous cries from downstairs—her pleas for assistance with her snowy TV screen or her insistence that she had heard a prowler. This time, however, her voice rose above the hi-fi upstairs in Joe's room, where we lay half-clothed and entwined in each other's limbs on the bed. Joe went to investigate. I sat up, pushing my outer and undergarments back into place, in the event that Jean herself might make a sudden appearance, which she sometimes did, unannounced, under some pretext of sociability.

I knew she was lonely, and I even liked her in her state of inebriated need. Something about her reminded me of my own speechless and inchoate desire. But I never knew what to say to her. She embarrassed me, so I avoided her, keeping our conversations to a polite minimum.

Joe hurried back, telling me that Jean was on the toilet in the little alcove downstairs, where she had fallen sideways against a windowpane and gashed her forehead. "Will you stay with her," he asked, "while I call an ambulance?" This was the last thing I wanted to do, but I couldn't see any way to refuse. I had no idea what I might encounter—no doubt some bloody, awful mess.

Jean was still sitting slumped on the toilet, with her pajama bottoms down around her feet, blubbering about dying. Suddenly I felt sorry for her and bent toward her, smoothing her thin, brown hair back from the open wound above her eyes.

"There, there," I said, as though she were a child who had run too hard, fallen, and skinned her knees. "Everything's going to be all right."

"Are you sure?" she said.

"Here, let's pull these up," I replied, reaching down to take hold of her pajama bottoms. "Now lift."

I didn't want Jean's thin, naked thighs exposed to the eyes of strangers. Only after making sure that she was covered did I think to hold something other than Kleenex to the profusely bleeding cut on her head. By now, my own hands were red and sticky, so I washed them carefully, then pressed a hand towel to her torn flesh.

Jean was moaning and distraught, yet somehow docile, as though she really believed I could comfort her. As though the long disaster of her life could be arrested and reversed in the here and now. For a moment I felt this also. More than anything, I wanted to be able to love her.

The paramedics arrived faster than I could have imagined—two young men, who had little patience for a sad-eyed, bourbon-mouthed, wobbly-legged woman. Jean responded by insisting on a cigarette before allowing herself to be taken—strapped down on a stretcher, like the emergency she was. Joe and I, feeling responsible for her, agreed to follow her to the hospital.

Once there, sitting in the waiting room, I began to shake. What if she had died, I wondered, imagining the situation as far worse than it was. What if she had bled to death, sitting on the toilet with me holding a sopping Kleenex to her head? Why didn't I think of the towel sooner? Why was I so concerned about lifting her pajama bottoms, smoothing her hair? But, thank goodness, now she was safe; she would be all right.

A crisis like this confronted me with my deepest fear. When my father died, I hadn't been able to help. At age nine, how could I have known what to do? There wasn't any 911 then, and besides we were nowhere near a telephone. My father drowned faster than you could wink an eye. Would I have tried to reach him if I had known he was in trouble? I didn't even know how to swim. But then, at least, I might have gone with him. I wouldn't have been left behind, feeling useless and empty.

Jean's distress aroused all my sleeping anxieties. In a situation of danger, I was afraid that I might fail to save a life. A chasm opened before me, like the one that yawned at my feet when I realized that no one could rescue my father.

I felt doubly grateful for Joe, whose presence of mind I admired. I credited him with saving Jean from her self-destructiveness and folly, if not from actually bleeding to death. I sat pressed against him in the car as we drove home.

Jean was sitting, comfortably bandaged and suddenly talkative in the back.

"You know what?" she said conspiratorially—as though we had shared some great adventure, and she was about to tell us what it meant. "You know what they thought at the hospital? They thought you were my children!" She laughed at the apparent absurdity of this mistake. But, as I turned to look at her, I caught a flash of satisfaction on her face.

Later, in Joe's room, I allowed him to undress me fully. We lay naked with each other in the dark, and as he felt down my body, I let my hands wander over his smooth, muscular chest and abdomen. There was nothing I wanted more than to reciprocate the pleasure I felt. I was having my period, but it didn't matter. We were ravenous for each other and careless.

I have replayed this moment in my mind many times, wondering what it was that allowed me, finally, to surrender. I believe it was Jean's crisis and Joe's response that tipped the scales, causing me to turn toward him, as much for safety and comfort as for sex. There was a grain of truth in what Jean said about our appearing to be her children. In her cries for help, she reminded me of my mother, whose need, though less overt, was equally real. If Joe knew how to handle Jean's SOS, perhaps he would also know what to do with mine.

When I was growing up, I looked to my older brother for comfort. As he entered adolescence, he began physically to resemble my father, whom I had idealized in my grief. What happened between us when I was thirteen, though limited in physical terms, nonetheless frightened me—enough to foreclose the possibility of sex until I met Joe. The story goes like this.

One lazy Saturday afternoon, we went bike riding together through the winding streets of our comfortable neighborhood. We stopped at a boarded-up house—one we used to think of as haunted, which was inhabited by an eccentric elderly man and his two sisters. The strangeness of this house seemed to evoke forbidden thoughts and fantasies. My brother began to talk about sex—remembering things we had done when we were younger. I didn't respond, but I also did not stop him. He continued, in this seductive way, when we got home. My mother was out; we were old enough, at this point, not to need a baby-sitter.

Why not undress? my brother suggested. Why not see what it is that adults do with each other? I was ambivalent, yet interested. Without actually saying yes, I began to comply. I went as far as removing my pedal pushers and underpants, while he took off his blue jeans and briefs. He held his penis and moved it against my vulva in a sultry, languorous motion—until I climaxed, at which point I felt suddenly terrified and ashamed. I wanted everything to stop and told him so. Hastily, I gathered up my clothes and left the room.

What had we done, I wondered? What if I became pregnant? Although I had not yet begun to menstruate, I didn't know enough to realize the unlikelihood of this possibility. I was a girl who did not want to acknowledge what was happening to her body—to the sprouting hairs on her pubis and under her arms, to the soft, plushy contours of her breasts. I preferred to play with dolls, pretending at motherhood with plastic and rubber, instead of attending to my brother's explicit and alarming instructions. At the same time, I had yielded—not enough for him to enter me, yet enough for him to make me come.

For years, I told myself that what my brother and I did was nothing like what I witnessed in Ford's play. Because he did not actually penetrate me, we were not guilty of incest. Yet I did have an orgasm, and in my confused and anxious state this was just as bad, if not worse. I couldn't claim that I had been victimized or seduced because I had partly enjoyed what we did. My pleasure meant that I had sinned and ought to be punished.

Although my first impulse was to confess my transgression—to anyone, even my mother—I didn't. I couldn't picture her reaction as anything but catastrophic. In time, the incident faded, along with my memory of the vividness of my response. As long as I didn't dwell on it, or allow myself to feel too much in the way of sexual excitement, I could maintain an image of myself as blameless.

By the time I went to see *The Cement Garden,* I could no longer sustain this self-image. On the contrary, I was having an affair, which challenged every preconception I had about myself. What I was doing with my lover felt forbidden, yet I persisted—a reminder of my long-ago attraction to my older brother. The pressure of this memory was such that I wanted, finally, to explore it, regardless of what I might find. In approaching the puzzle of incest, I was beginning to confront the riddle of myself.

Although I did not succeed in unraveling the mystery of my affair at this time, I did understand one thing about Julie and Jack. They were not just succumbing to the force of ungovernable desire, they were consoling each other in the face of their double bereavement. This insight helped me to forgive myself for my behavior at thirteen, but it did not resolve my dilemma in the present. The missing link— the piece having specifically to do with sex—came into focus much later, when I remembered Ford's play and my relationship with my graduate-school boyfriend.

It wasn't only comfort I was seeking, I was also looking for a hidden access route to my past. It was my dad I kept looking for and the trauma of his loss that I relived each time I found him in a lover. The stronger my desire and the more pleasure I felt, the more terrified I was. Like Annabella and Giovanni,

I felt that my history was tragic. I didn't know how to act on my desire and survive it.

Oedipal desire—the erotic attraction that parents and children feel for each other—must be repressed, Freud says, in order for civilization to develop. The alternative is disastrous. Without having read Freud, I believed this in my heart of hearts. But I took things one step further. Loving my father as I had and having lost him made all love feel forbidden to me and incestuous.

I wanted the same thing Giovanni wants, a state of fusion so intense that the boundary between self and other is dissolved. Yet every time I approached this experience I drew back. Until I fell into an affair so absorbing that my body responded in spite of myself. Each time I came, I was thrown into a state of such physical and emotional confusion that I felt it necessary, finally, to end the relationship.

I'm not talking here about infidelity, but about something sadder and more elusive. I'm talking about a girl so in love with her father that she could not bear to lose—or to recover—him in another man. A girl who could not grow up. Each time she took a chance on love, she found herself face-to-face with a part of herself she could not assimilate. Such a girl has no need for external sanction or control. She will find a way to punish herself.

What is it about sex, I wonder, that awakens our deepest, most powerful—and often unresolved—emotions? And why, as a culture, do we attempt to deny this awareness, treating sex as though it were a matter of hedonism or hygiene, a function of the body that does not engage the whole of one's history and selfhood? Turning this around, we might say that it is our sexual behavior that reveals us most fully, divulging even the secrets we keep from ourselves, confessing who we really are.

From the Center
1994–1997

Surrender:

Shadowlands

No one ever told me that grief felt so like fear.

— C. S. Lewis, *A Grief Observed*

RECENTLY, I ENCOUNTERED a surprising statistic regarding the state of orphanhood. According to the U.S. census from 1930 onward, approximately 5 percent of the population suffers the loss of a parent before the age of eighteen. I was shocked when I discovered this fact. Surely, I thought, the percentage must be higher—as of course it would be in earlier centuries or in less developed countries. I was startled to realize that my own peacetime, middle-of-America, 1950s reality was so little shared. For me, it was everything. It shaped my world.

The universe I inhabited after my father's death was a place of terror. If my dad could disappear in a flash, anything could happen. Accidents, natural disasters, any kind of catastrophe, I felt, was normal. Even expected. You never knew when the next dreadful thing would occur. It was best to be on your guard. That way, braced for the worst, you might not be so annihilated.

Years later, I had a glimpse of the state of mind that descended on me, like a blazing meteor from the sky, as a child. I was visiting my mother in St. Louis with my daughter Jessica, who was then about five years old. Driving home from the airport in a light rain, we were rear-ended in a chain-reaction accident, caused by a car stalled somewhere ahead of us on the highway. No one but my mother, whose right knee had been pushed into the dashboard, was seriously hurt. As I stepped out of the car, intending to exchange insurance information with the drivers in front and behind, I felt projected into a reality so alien that I could hardly recognize my surroundings. I don't remember ever being more frightened than I was at that moment—standing in the wet dark, in the middle of an interstate highway with cars whizzing by on either side. It was like being transported into a novel by Stephen King. I felt both hunted and haunted, like one of those characters who are doomed from the start in a grade B sci-fi movie. Later, when I recounted this story to the therapist I was seeing, he said, "Maybe this is how you felt when your dad died."

I had already read *A Grief Observed,* C. S. Lewis's account of his bereavement over the death of his wife Joy Davidman Gresham, when I saw *Shadowlands,* Richard Attenborough's film version of their romance, in the winter of 1994. The film deals with the short period in Lewis's life that spanned their relationship—from their first meeting, to their marriage, Joy's cancer diagnosis, remission, and death. Several points in this story brought me to the verge of tears. By the end, when the film shows Lewis attempting to comfort his stepson Douglas, I gave up my struggle for control and broke down crying. While I wasn't the only person in the movie theater wiping her eyes, I felt a special resonance with this story. How much of it was "true," I wondered. And why was I so susceptible? To answer this question, I felt that I needed to know more about Lewis himself. I was especially curious about how he had come to fall so deeply and fully in love so late in life. What were the steps leading to this moment? I began to explore his biography.

Almost immediately I discovered that Lewis and I had each suffered the death of a parent in childhood. We were even the same age (nine years old). Lewis lost his mother to cancer, an event he describes in vivid detail in his spiritual autobiography *Surprised by Joy*.

> There came a night when I was ill and crying both with headache and toothache and distressed because my mother did not come to me. That was because she was ill too; and what was odd was that there were several doctors in her room, and voices and comings and goings all over the house and doors shutting and opening. It seemed to last for hours. And then my father, in tears, came into my room and began to try to convey to my terrified mind things it had never conceived before. It was in fact cancer and followed the usual course; an operation (they operated in the patient's house in those days), an apparent convalescence, a return of the disease, increasing pain, and death.

His father, Lewis says succinctly "never fully recovered from this loss." As a result, Lewis and his brother Warren (called Warnie) drew closer—but at the cost of their isolation from their father, the sight of whose "adult misery and adult terror" paralyzed and alienated them.

The more I read about Lewis, the more I became convinced that we were alike—at least in our experience of grief. While clearly an imaginative and precocious child, Lewis lost some piece of his feeling self in the aftermath of this traumatic event. He also lost the rudiments of a religious faith. "When her case was pronounced hopeless," he says, "I remembered what I had been taught; that prayers offered in faith would be granted." Cruelly, this childish belief was dashed. When his prayers for his mother's recovery from cancer proved ineffectual, he shifted ground, trusting in a miracle. When this much-desired transformation did not take place, the boy

Lewis cut his spiritual losses, dropping God like a hot potato. Not willing to admit the depth of his pain and disillusion, he says that this "disappointment produced no results beyond itself. The thing hadn't worked, but I was used to things not working, and I thought no more about it." Even as an adult, Lewis seems not to want to acknowledge the gravity of this moment. Yet, in the very coolness of his disavowal, I sense the dimensions of his boyhood pain.

For Lewis, the death of his mother caused "all settled happiness, all that was tranquil and reliable" to disappear from his life. It was as though he had lost the very ground beneath his feet. "It was sea and islands now," he writes, "the great continent had sunk like Atlantis." Where once he had no special concern for the future, no need to watch his step, now he was in a state of anxiety.

As bereaved children, of course, we do not use such language. The state of fear we live in is so timeless and pervasive as to have no name. Because it seems to have sprung from nowhere, it appears to have no end. It is not separable from the self—like a real danger or threat. It is a form of internal weather rather, a condition of being. While a philosopher might invent a phrase like "ontological insecurity" or "existential angst" to help neutralize this kind of terror, a child has no such resource. Without the assistance of some kindly adult, we are at the mercy of our inner turmoil. We are linguistically and emotionally at sea.

I, too, lost faith as a child, though I can't pinpoint this moment in time. Nothing in my behavior as a good little Catholic girl changed. I continued to confess my sins, go to Mass and take communion, even to sing in the church choir, as the nuns at my school and priests in my parish exhorted. But this round of familiar activity was now infected with a feeling of dreary necessity that killed any pleasure I might have experienced earlier. I continued to pray and examine my con-science, but without the energy or conviction of belief. Like Lewis, I was used to things not working. God was no longer a benevolent gift giver, a kindly Santa Claus in the sky, but rather a vague and oppressive nonentity, like a gray-white fog spread over everything. I did not imagine that anyone heard my prayers or that they made any difference. At best, I prayed out of habit, at worst out of resignation.

Slowly, my heart was hardening. There came a moment when I felt nothing but irritation at the ritual requirements of my faith: abstinence from meat on Friday, attendance at Mass on Sunday, confession before communion, all under pain of mortal sin. There was no satisfaction or pleasure in it. Rather, I felt hedged round with prohibitions and threat. The years of submission to this spiritless regimen had taken their toll. By the time I went away to college, I felt there was no point in continuing. I had become indifferent.

Lewis downplays his disillusion with God for not performing a miracle to save his mother's life. He even seems to blame himself for not having true religious faith, for approaching God "without love, without awe, even without fear," regard-ing him "merely as a magician." "I imagine that a 'faith' of this kind is often generated in children," he says stiffly, "and that its disappointment is of no religious importance." Turn-ing his back on the frightened child who must have poured his whole soul into a plea for his mother's cure, Lewis pre-tends that he wasn't much surprised at God's lack of response. Yet who can love such a heartless deity? He seems more de-serving of hate. Later in life, after Lewis had recovered his faith and converted to Christianity, he tried to address this knotty problem.

In *The Problem of Pain,* published in 1940 (twelve years before he met Joy Gresham), Lewis labors to justify the necessity for human suffering—with rather chilling results. God emerges from Lewis's portrait as a strict disciplinarian who inflicts pain on his subjects for the sake of their moral improvement. God truly loves us, Lewis argues, but we are not especially deserving of this love. "Man, as a species, spoiled himself," he explains, so that "good, to us in our present state, must therefore mean primarily remedial or corrective good." Unfortunately, Lewis associates such corrective action with "the older type of nurse or parent," who was "quite right in thinking that the first step in education is 'to break the child's will.'"

From what Lewis himself tells us, his father's irrationality in the aftermath of his wife Flora's death was extreme. "Under the pressure of anxiety," Lewis writes, his father's "temper became incalculable." He "spoke wildly and acted unjustly," terrifying his grief-stricken boys. "Thus by a peculiar cruelty of fate," Lewis relates, his father "had he but known it, was really losing his sons as well as his wife." Lewis's reference to a child's self-will as a "bitter, prolonged rage at every thwarting," as even a "black, Satanic wish to kill or die rather than to give in," seems as relevant a description of his father's emotional temper as his own. Whose will, in such an unequal power struggle, is to be broken?

I believe that Lewis was struggling to comprehend his own history. What sense could he make of his mother's agonizing pain and death? Why should a child be so deprived of his primary source of nurturance? Why should he be left with a father so self-absorbed that he could not respond to the needs of his sons? Within a month of their mother's death, both Lewis and his brother Warnie were banished from their Belfast family home to a rather brutally administered English public school—from which they regularly begged for release. When Lewis turned his face back to God it was not out of a conviction of divine compassion, but rather one of brute submission.

I held out longer. I hated the idea of a God who knew only how to reprimand, humiliate, or punish. I withheld belief as a primitive way of returning the pain I felt. Silence, I understood obscurely, was the surest way of expressing resentment. Where love was denied, I would deny love back. God was like an irrational parent, whose rage against me I could not even begin to fathom. In retaliation, I shut him out. I would serve him some of his own medicine; I would close my heart.

What I felt as a bleak absence or void in my life corresponded to the hole in my heart left by my father's departure. If God was so all-powerful and good, why hadn't he saved me from such a disaster? What could I have done to deserve such a willful act of cruelty? Who would want to hurt a child like that?

It's harder, I think, to be angry at real people than to be angry at a deity so removed and impervious as to be immune to the effects of one's rage. No doubt I was furious with my dad for leaving me the way he did—as if he couldn't care less. I was even more angry with my mother, who seemed so near, yet so distant. Why couldn't she notice me? Because she was the only protector I had, I couldn't afford to lose her. I could not allow myself to be upset with my one remaining parent. It was much easier to be ticked off at God.

Lewis very perceptively describes how it felt not to believe in God. "I maintained that God did not exist," he states. "I was also very angry with God for not existing. I was equally angry with Him for creating a world." A true atheist would be at peace with God's nonbeing, I think. It is like a child to be furious.

How does one stop feeling angry about a loss as absolute and devastating as the death of a parent? Such a deprivation feels like a permanent, hence unforgivable, act of betrayal. At the same time, raging against God brings no relief. Anger breeds anger, like the escalating violence of a hurricane. Rarely, moreover, does God deign to respond—as he does to Job, addressing him directly from the center of the whirlwind. More often than not, we muddle along, cherishing our bitterness and resentment, until some fortuitous sequence of events offers release.

In many respects, I was lucky. Although my family was dispersed in the aftermath of my father's death (my grandparents, aunt, and two uncles left town), it was not completely dysfunctional. My mother rallied and managed to carry on. Our economic circumstances were difficult, but we were not desperately poor. When my mother remarried, we achieved some semblance of emotional and material stability—for a few years at least. There were periods of respite for me in my anxiety about what life means or has to offer. I was smart enough to go to a good college and get a solid liberal arts education. When I married for the first time, I chose a man whose extended family would provide a safe haven for the child I wanted, but didn't yet know I would conceive. My second marriage gave me experiences of real pleasure and joy. Something within was moving me toward things that I wanted without my knowing how or why.

In Lewis's case, two life changes seem to have contributed to the lessening of his hurt—his forming a household with the mother of his friend Patrick Moore, who died in the trenches of World War I, and the death of his irascible father ten years later. Lewis and his Oxford undergraduate friend had agreed at the outset of the war that if one of them died the other would look after the surviving parent. For the motherless

Lewis, the assumption of such a responsibility was more of a blessing than a burden. From 1919 until her death in 1951, Lewis lived with Patrick's mother Janie Moore, in a domestic arrangement that may have included sexual relations. Though barely twenty-one, Lewis found himself a head of household, in charge of the welfare of a woman in her forties, who was also raising a daughter. Lewis's relationship with Mrs. Moore, while no doubt complex and surely ambiguous in regard to his role as surrogate son or husband, seems to have given him something that the purely intellectual atmosphere of Oxford could not, a position of importance in a stable family order and the comfort of home.

In 1930, Lewis consolidated his domestic situation by pooling funds with Janie and his brother Warnie to buy The Kilns, an English cottage set on several acres of ground that included a small woods, pond, and garden. Lewis's biographer A. N. Wilson speculates that he took advantage of his conversion to Christianity in the following year to end his sexual involvement with Mrs. Moore. Whatever the nature of this relation had been, everyone seems to agree that Lewis was devoted to this rather demanding, but also vivacious and affectionate, woman. Most likely, she gave Lewis a feeling of being appreciated and warmly cared for that he had lacked from early childhood. With the death of his father in 1929, Lewis seems to have experienced another kind of relief.

Albert Lewis's violent reaction to his wife's death permanently scarred his relationship with his sons. Writing about this period in his fifties, Lewis conveys the hostility instilled in him by the spectacle of his father's bereavement. "His nerves had never been of the steadiest and his emotions had always been uncontrolled," Lewis states. As a result, Lewis and his brother came "to rely more and more exclusively on each other for all that made life bearable; to have confidence only in each other." The orphaned boys, who lost one parent to death and the other to a self-absorbed grief, "drew daily closer together . . . two frightened urchins huddled for warmth in a bleak world." Lewis was as angry with his father as he was with God.

Lewis's recovery of religious faith follows so closely on his father's death that the two events seem interrelated. It's as though the loss of his father killed his childhood rage. Within a year, he experienced a change of heart so profound as to amount to a religious conversion. This process, as Lewis describes it, was felt as a lowering of resistance (not unlike the cessation of anger) and a corresponding feeling of release. "I became aware that I was holding something at bay," he says, "or shutting something out. Or, if you like, that I was wearing some stiff clothing, like corsets, or even a suit of armor, as if I were a lobster." Lewis felt that he had a choice. "I could open the door or I could keep it shut; I could unbuckle the armor or keep it on." Without fanfare, or even a sense of calculated risk, Lewis took the more dangerous course. He describes this movement of the soul in language that is curiously detached. "The choice appeared to be momentous," he says, "but it was also strangely unemotional. I was moved by no desires or fears. In a sense I was not moved by anything." Yet, almost immediately he experienced a "repercussion on the imaginative level." "I felt as if I were a man of snow at long last beginning to melt," he states. "The melting was starting in my back—drip-drip and presently trickle-trickle." Somewhat unnerved by this development, he confesses, "I rather disliked the feeling."

Lewis experiences his conversion first as a kind of interior rain. Not being used to such a sensation, he can only describe it as something inside him melting. He does not think of himself as weeping. Yet reading Lewis's account of his inner transformation, I cannot help associating it with the boy whose grief had no sanction or outlet in childhood. At long last, I imagine, he was able to cry.

I can't locate the precise moment at which I began to relinquish my rage against God. For me, this process was neither dramatic nor instantaneous, but rather gradual, taking place over a number of years. As my life began to develop some stability through work, marriage, friendship, and motherhood, my sense of imminent catastrophe abated. I began to feel less at the mercy of my world, both inner and outer. While still jittery, as if poised for flight, I felt on the whole less anxious. I began to experience moments of calm, brief flashes of pleasure, even happiness. I thought of them as oases of the spirit, gifts that I did not deserve but which I relished, like manna descending on me from the hard blue of a desert sky. Obscurely, I felt the need to place these feelings in some kind of framework.

At first, I was merely aware of a desire to sit in a church by myself. Then, I found myself wanting to explore religious denominations other than Catholicism—though I was distinctly wary of dogma. One winter, I tried attending the services of a local Unitarian society, thinking that if I could eliminate the obvious trappings of Christianity that I would be able to find something of use. Later, veering back toward the comfort of the familiar, I went to a Catholic church that celebrated the (now mostly defunct) Latin Mass. None of these impulses was sustained for very long. I would lurch in one direction, then another, returning from each excursion to the burrow of my skepticism and unbelief.

Slowly, I felt a lessening of resistance. I wasn't so much angry with God at this point as sorrowful. I no longer felt him as specifically vengeful toward me, but rather as removed, somehow indifferent to my fate. He didn't mean me

166   ➤   *Crying at the Movies*

any harm; he was just not paying attention. He wasn't at home, or at least not taking calls.

There came a time when I felt the need for the kind of spiritual sustenance that I associated with my early practice of religion, yet was stymied by the task of translating this need into my adult experience. There were so many things I no longer believed in that I could hardly imagine becoming a member of any organized religion. In particular, if I didn't assent to the idea of heaven, hell, or purgatory, was unsure about the divinity of Christ, never went to confession or even considered any of my transgressions "mortal," how could I claim a place in the Catholic Church? And if I tried, wouldn't I run up against that ultimate figure of disapproval, the Pope? No, I felt, there were simply too many obstacles to be overcome. Perhaps I didn't belong in such company. While I did not consider myself damned by this conclusion, neither did I feel blessed.

Once again, my attitude shifted. Although this next development proved critical, at the time it felt rather ordinary and uneventful. One day, it dawned on me that the Pope himself would never know what I thought. This realization freed me to follow my impulse—to go to church whenever I wanted and take from this experience what I most needed. Without quite knowing what I was doing, I was seeking God.

Lewis's removal of spiritual armor and surrender to faith led to other transformations in his life. The year following his recovery of a belief in God, he converted to Christianity. An outpouring of books followed. From the 1930s to the early 1950s, Lewis was busy publishing works of scholarship, religious apologetics, and children's fiction. He also became a popular public speaker and BBC lecturer. It's as though something in his sensibility began to coalesce, leading to an extraordinary period of creativity. This development was, I believe, as much psychological in nature as it was spiritual.

How does a disintegrated personality heal itself, I wonder? Is it a matter of individual constitution, external environment, or pure dumb luck? Or some felicitous combination of all of the above? In Lewis's case, circumstances seemed to conspire with his personality and intelligence to allay his childhood anguish and to allow some form of psychic renewal. His happy discovery of a mothering figure in Janie Moore, along with his ability to create an idiosyncratic family with the persons at hand—Janie, her daughter Maureen, and his brother Warnie—seems to have provided the kind of security Lewis needed in order to allow him to explore the terra incognita of his boyhood loss. This is what I see him doing in his most compelling literary achievement, the stories he wrote for children, set in the never-never land of Narnia.

In the Narnia chronicles, Lewis creates a magical (and sometimes mystical) realm peopled with witches, talking animals, and a particularly magisterial lion named Aslan. The children who find themselves transported to this world bring with them some very real-life dilemmas, including questions about death. While central to the answers he provides, Lewis's Christian faith never seems obtrusive or heavy-handed. Rather, the suspension of belief in a totally rational universe that informs a religious view of life blends seamlessly into the atmosphere of wonder associated with the fairy-tale genre.

It's one thing to allow that God might exist and that he might even wish us well. It's quite another to live out the consequences of such a belief in moments of pain, anxiety, or terror. Or maybe it's the other way around. Perhaps the capacity to believe is an index of the kind of inner scaffolding we need in order to withstand the psychic assault of grief? As a child, I had neither the internal nor the external structure of security that would allow me to experience the full impact of my loss. I was too scared to mourn.

Reflecting on how we labor to avoid sadness, the poet Rainer Maria Rilke writes: "It seems to me that almost all our sadnesses are moments of tension, which we feel as paralysis because we no longer hear our astonished emotions." When we are bereaved as children, it is especially hard to withstand the clamor of our outraged feelings—they are so insistent and cacophonous that we go temporarily deaf, shattering our eardrums in self-defense. Even for adults, such a state of internal noise is challenging, as Rilke observes, "because we are alone with the unfamiliar presence that has entered us; because everything we trust and are used to is for a moment taken away from us; because we stand in the midst of a transition where we cannot remain standing." Having faith is a little like feeling ground beneath our feet, even (or especially) when we are not looking down.

When does such a conviction become an indwelling thing, rather than a desperate search for something outside of the self? How does a child whose universe disintegrates as a result of the death of a parent recover a feeling of trust and ease of being in the world? The psychoanalyst Melanie Klein, writing about the slow process of mourning, refers to the task of rebuilding "with anguish the inner world, which is felt to be in danger of deteriorating and collapsing." For Lewis, as for me, this labor stretched over decades, proceeding at such a snail's pace that its effects were all but invisible. Perhaps there is no adequate explanation for a process we might simply call healing. Yet something like this can and does occur—the irony being that the outcome of a successful mourning prepares us for even greater emotional risk, deeper loss.

Attenborough's *Shadowlands* offers us an image of the labor of loving with the full self, that is to say, with an adult awareness of the inevitability of suffering. William Nicholson's screenplay assimilates the basic features of Lewis's biography, giving us a distilled portrait of a man who chooses, against the odds of his settled, donnish existence, to give himself unreservedly to a woman whose life he knows to be ending. We witness, in a sense, the culmination of Lewis's history—beginning with the early loss of his mother and flight into intellectual pursuits, including the relaxation of his defenses through his relationship with Janie Moore, his recovery of religious faith and subsequent release of creativity. It's as though everything in his life prepared him for this final emotional epiphany and surrender. The believability of this transformation is due, in part, to the exceptional performances of Debra Winger and Anthony Hopkins under Attenborough's graceful direction, but also to the psychological resonance of Nicholson's script.

The film achieves its visual and narrative effects modestly—through a few simple settings, repetitions of scene and encounter among the main characters, and heavy reliance on medium and close shots. The few long shots Attenborough permits himself underscore the film's basic themes, contrasting the cloistered atmosphere of Oxford (viewed from a distance as a medieval town sufficient unto itself) with the open, emotionally suffused landscape of Golden Valley in the Herefordshire countryside. Other, more domestic settings include: The Kilns, Lewis's warrenlike home; his rooms at Oxford, and his favorite pub; Joy's apartment and her hospital room. We keep returning to these environments, with a deepening appreciation for the meanings contained in each, as the drama of Lewis's relationship with Joy unfolds.

Three settings are particularly resonant: the attic at Kilns, Golden Valley, and Joy's hospital room. The dramatic encounters that take place in these locations are responsible for the film's extraordinary emotional impact. By the end of the film, it is no surprise that most of the audience is in tears.

Attenborough prepares us for our first sight of the attic at Kilns with an exchange between Lewis and his Oxford cronies at his favorite pub. Defending himself against the charge that the entrance into Narnia through a wardrobe filled with fur coats in *The Lion, the Witch and the Wardrobe* contains Freudian allusions to the "fur" on a woman's body, Lewis demonstrates the action of a child pushing through the coats to the door at the back. "It's just magic," he insists, meaning that it has nothing to do with sex. Later, when Joy and her son Douglas arrive at The Kilns to visit Lewis, Douglas brings his worn copy of *The Lion, the Witch and the Wardrobe* to be signed by Lewis, who writes somewhat glibly, "The magic never ends." "Well if it does, sue him," Joy retorts. Twice, Douglas ventures into the attic to view the actual wardrobe that inspired Lewis's fantasy creation. The second time, he musters his courage to explore its contents, eagerly pushing aside the heavy wool coats in anticipation of discovering an opening into the magical world of Narnia. Surprised by the sudden appearance of Lewis, Douglas tries to disguise his disappointment at finding an ordinary clothes closet by saying, "I knew it was just an old wardrobe."

The scenes dealing with Joy's cancer treatment, remission, and death echo not only Lewis's long-ago experience of his mother's death from cancer, but also allude to *The Magician's Nephew*, where Lewis's protagonist Digory seeks a magical remedy for his mother's illness in the land of Narnia. In this story, Digory is tempted to steal an "apple of life" in order to cure his mother's cancer. After resisting this temptation, he confesses his forbidden desire to Aslan, who gives him permission to pluck one of the magic apples to take home to England. "It will not, in your world, give endless life," he cautions, "but it will heal." Through the medium of fiction— where all things are possible—Lewis allows Digory to accomplish what his own desperate prayers could not. The son saves his mother's life.

The odd thing about this wish-fulfilling fantasy is that it appears to take place in Joy's hospital room. While Attenborough downplays the reference to Lewis's exploration of this fantasy in *The Magician's Nephew,* he picks up on screenwriter Nicholson's intuition that Joy's remission is due to some combination of Lewis's prayers, her son's heartfelt wish, and the "magic" inherent in mature, reciprocal love. The hospital scenes owe their power to the effectiveness with which Hopkins and Winger express such love for each other. Perhaps the most moving moment occurs in the course of Lewis's proposal to marry Joy for a second time— in a religious (as opposed to civil) ceremony. After declaring somewhat awkwardly, "I'm going to marry you, Joy. I'm going to marry you before God and the world," he proposes to her formally, as she requests. "Will you marry this foolish, frightened, old man, who needs you more than he can bear to say and loves you even though he hardly knows how?" Lewis asks, leaning toward her exhausted, reclining form. "Just this once," Joy replies.

The near-deathbed quality of this scene is surely one of its emotional triggers, yet this is no twenty-something *Love Story.* The protagonists are middle-aged and experienced. They know what the stakes are. They are exactly aware of what they have to love, cherish, and enjoy—and to lose.

Whatever magic love (or a child's ardent wish for his mother's survival) performs, it is temporary. Joy's fate has long ago been sealed. While we may not know her real life story on viewing this film for the first time, we can guess at it. Her remission is unhoped for and hence miraculous, but it won't last. "Can't you do something?" Douglas asks Lewis, some months later, as he watches his mother being carried out of the house on a stretcher. "I'm afraid not," Lewis replies.

The trip to Golden Valley is an invention—a conflation of Lewis and Joy's honeymoon trip to Ireland and an excursion to Greece they made shortly before Joy's death. Yet the emotional truth conveyed by this episode resonates powerfully with what we know of Lewis's life from his writings, while clearly foreshadowing the concluding events of the film.

Golden Valley is introduced into the narrative through a conversation between Joy and Lewis on her first visit to The Kilns. An idyllic scene in the tradition of nineteenth-century landscape painting, it hangs in Lewis's study, a relic from his childhood nursery. It's a "view of heaven," he explains to Joy, not a depiction of an actual locale. Interestingly, this conversation shades into Lewis's admission to Joy that he had once been "really hurt"—by his mother's death. If Golden Valley represents a view of heaven, it is a fictional, faraway place, one from which Lewis was exiled at an early age, and to which he can only aspire through the balletics of faith. Late in the film, Joy challenges, "Let's go look for it, Jack."

Golden Valley, it turns out, really exists, but it doesn't mean "golden," which (as the innkeeper explains) is an English bastardization of the Welsh word for "west." Finding themselves at last in this green and sun-drenched landscape, Joy and Lewis come up against the reality of their situation. When Lewis professes his deep contentment in the moment, avowing that he is no longer "waiting for anything new to happen," Joy forces a confrontation. "It's not going to last, Jack," she says bluntly, "I'm going to die." Overriding Lewis's objection that such an admission will spoil their pleasure in the present, Joy pushes ahead. "It doesn't spoil it, it makes it real," she insists, explaining further that "the pain then is part of the happiness now. That's the deal."

Some months later, her remission ended, Joy is forced to return to the hospital for more radiation treatments. The period of healing and happiness, though genuine, is limited in duration. While Golden Valley may provide a view of heaven, there is no "forever after." This time, when Joy returns home, it is to die.

In Joy's last hours, Lewis confesses his helplessness at the thought of his impending loss. "I don't know what to do, Joy," he says. "You'll have to tell me what to do." Ever the realist, she whispers, "You have to let me go, Jack," to which Lewis replies, "I'm not sure that I can." As Joy closes her eyes, Lewis speaks to her directly: "I love you, Joy. I love you so much. You've made me so happy. I didn't know I could be so happy. You're the truest person I've ever known. Sweet Jesus, be with my beloved wife, Joy. Forgive me if I love her too much. Have mercy on us both." In the next frame, Douglas wakes abruptly, sitting bolt upright in bed. His mother has just died. In the chain of loss, he has inherited the experience that Lewis himself underwent as a child.

I'm not sure how central Lewis's belief in an afterlife was to his religious faith, which appears to survive Joy's death, but in a bruised and darkened form. That his grief was real and profound, even heretical in its questioning of God's intent in permitting such suffering, is clear from the personal journal he kept, documenting the stages of his mourning. Early on, he muses, "The conclusion I dread is not, 'So there's no God after all,' but 'So this is what God's really like.'" Later, he extends this train of thought: "If God's goodness is inconsistent with hurting us, then either God is not good or there is no God: for in the only life we know He hurts us beyond our worst fears and beyond all we can imagine." Still later, he offers the sardonic comment: "Someone said, I believe, 'God always geometrizes.' Supposing the truth were 'God always vivisects'?" With a sense of horror, Lewis admits that he cannot even pray for Joy. When he tries, "Bewilderment and amazement come over me. I have a ghastly sense of unreality, of speaking into a vacuum about a nonentity." Where is she now, he wonders? If she is not a body, in what sense does she exist? If she is "with God," as well-meaning friends would have him believe, what does this mean? "You never know how much you really believe anything until its truth or falsehood becomes a matter of life and death to you," he admits candidly. "Only a real risk tests the reality of a belief."

What Lewis's loss calls forth from him is not primarily a renewal of religious faith or even a statement about the existence of an afterlife, but rather an awareness of what adult love requires. "Bereavement," he affirms, "is a universal and integral part of our experience of love. It follows marriage as normally as marriage follows courtship or as autumn follows summer. It is not a truncation of the process but one of its phases; not the interruption of the dance, but the next figure." Putting this another way, as Joy does in *Shadowlands*, "the pain then is part of the happiness now. That's the deal."

Love and suffering are intertwined, and mere human prayer cannot change this reality. In the most powerfully affecting scene in the film, Lewis confides this knowledge to his stepson Douglas, whom he finds sitting in the attic, staring disconsolately at the distinctly un-magic wardrobe.

"When I was your age," Lewis tells him, "my mother died. That was cancer, too. I thought that if I prayed for her to get better, and if I really believed she'd get better, then she wouldn't die. But she did."

"It doesn't work," Douglas responds dully.

"No. It doesn't work."

"I don't see why she had to get sick."

"Nor I."

There is no note of moral uplift here, no attempt to justify or explain—only an acknowledgment of mutual helplessness and loss. The next piece of dialogue underscores this painful reality. When asked point-blank whether he believes in heaven, Lewis replies, "Yes."

"I don't believe in heaven," Douglas rejoins.

"That's OK," says Lewis.

"I sure would like to see her again," Douglas persists, giving simultaneous expression to his wishfulness and despair.

"Me too," confesses Lewis, who suddenly loses his composure, breaking down into open sobs. As if tears were contagious, Douglas also begins to cry, reaching instinctively for the comfort of Lewis's large body. Huddled together on the attic stairs, both give way to their sorrow.

When Lewis says, "Me too," I responded in kind. His (and Douglas's) sorrow blended with mine in a way that felt immediate and real. Watching Lewis, a reserved, middle-aged man, give way to his grief, gave me permission to accept— and to express—my own.

What is remarkable about this scene is its head-on confrontation with the issue of loss. There is no attempt to sweeten or sentimentalize the process of mourning by implying that it is anything less than it is, a personal agony that is only relieved by feeling the pain—and perhaps sharing it. The sole consolation that *Shadowlands* offers is the kind that one human being can offer another, in this case the empathy that Lewis extends toward a boy in whom he recognizes some version of himself, both through his own childhood experience and his present loss. What Lewis gives Douglas is what he and his brother Warnie were denied, the comfort of adult understanding, which, in turn, confers the blessing of emotional release.

Sadness averted, Rilke writes, may do much harm. Such a sadness becomes "life that is unlived, rejected, lost, life that we can die of." A wiser course, he suggests, would be to "bear our sadnesses with greater trust than we have in our joys. For they are the moments when something new has entered us, something unknown." Yet the task that Rilke outlines is truly daunting, a labor of the spirit that can feel more exhausting than transformative. Rilke refers to sadness as a presence, like a guest who enters a room, but sadness more commonly gives rise to feelings of emptiness or fear. The vacuum that a death leaves in its wake, as Lewis graphically reports, is visceral. Though not literally afraid, he experiences "the same fluttering in my stomach, the same restlessness, the yawning." "I keep on swallowing," he notes—as if to combat an absence within.

Having spent most of my life trying to evade sadness, I can testify to the futility of such an effort. At the same time, I cannot quite bring myself to welcome grief. Instead, I have been trying to outrun my loss, as if my survival depended on outmaneuvering a wily adversary who may be temporarily given the slip, but never completely shaken off. Not too long ago, however, I caught of glimpse of what it might mean to incorporate, rather than to expel the feeling of aching hollowness that inhabits me when I dwell on my father's death.

Until recently, I have chosen to "forget" that my dad died in the month of August, feeling instead a mounting sense of dread that often culminates in an outburst of anger as the anniversary day draws near. In the last year or so, I have tried to focus my feelings of distress, to locate their source and put them back, so to speak, where they belong. Not having been allowed as a child to attend my father's funeral, I now improvise a memorial service of my own. On August 30, the day of his death—no matter where I am or what I am doing—I set aside some time to commemorate his loss.

A few years ago, I was on the road at the end of August, driving through Canada northwest of Toronto, on my way home to Minneapolis. On the afternoon of the 30th, I began looking for a place near water to stop for the night. The best bet, according to my map, looked like Parry Sound, a small town on an inlet of Georgian Bay. I was hoping to find a motel with a view. When nothing materialized fitting this description, my spirits began to sink. It was already late in the day, and Parry Sound was the only town of any size within a radius of a hundred miles. At last, I spied a crudely lettered sign pointing down a dirt road toward a place called "Woodland Resort." I followed this route past a small marina, through many twists and turns, until I arrived at a rustic lodge deep in a stand of pines, which did indeed look out over the water. A kindly older couple welcomed me and showed me the one remaining room—with a balcony and a view! Returning from dinner in town, I descended a short trail to the floating dock owned by the resort.

At first I sat on a bench, watching the last vestiges of sunset. Then, as it grew dark, I walked out onto the dock and lay down on my back. Small wavelets rocked me, giving me the illusion of lying in a canoe or rowboat. Though suspended over the water, I felt held by it, almost cradled in it. By now, the shoreline was a shape of blackness, the sky an inky blue. Here and there a light flashed over the water, signaling the late return of a boat to the marina. No one, I was sure, could see me lying flat on the dock, so close as to blend into its mass, itself hardly distinguishable from the water. Suddenly, I felt like talking to my dad. Not in my head, as if to an interior image or memory, but out loud, as if he were alive and real, somewhere out there in the darkness, listening.

"I miss you," I said. "I miss you so much, even now, after all this time. I love you, just as much as I did then. Maybe it seems odd to you that I'm so old—older than you—but it doesn't to me. I still want you back." It was OK, I thought, to talk like this. I knew that I was alone, but I didn't feel lonely. I sensed my dad's presence, as you might perceive a mist or fog on the horizon, evaporating and dispersing even as you look. How would he know how I felt unless I spoke to him directly? I wanted him to linger awhile longer.

I told him about my life—the things that I was proud of as well as the things that had gone wrong. I said I was sorry for ignoring him for so many years, especially for trying to obliterate the day of his death. I wanted him not to feel abandoned in the other world he had gone to. I promised I would take care of his memory, not by visiting his grave, but by keeping a piece of him inside me, the way some people create shrines in their homes, with photographs, flowers, and candles. "Don't worry," I said, "I won't forget you."

I had a sudden image for the vow I was making, which seemed perfectly natural, even inevitable, to me at the time. Maybe it was inspired by the setting, the feeling of being adrift, yet also anchored, on the water—as close as I could get to my dad's spirit, which I have always associated with the powerful Mississippi. As I lay on the dock in the warm and secret darkness, I felt my body as a space of hollowness that did not feel depleted or empty. It was like a vase, rather, or like a viola or cello, a container resonant with its own lack. I felt light with this awareness, even buoyant, the way I do when I swim to the center of some calm lake and float, arching my back and opening my arms to the sky. I feel my lungs then for the simple inflation devices that they are, gently expanding and contracting like small balloons, my body rising and falling in rhythm with my breath. It is this motion, this soft sift of air, taken in and released, that holds me at such moments in the water's liquid embrace.

For the first time, I felt my father, not absent, but as a part of me, something like a ghost presence, inhabiting the very space his departure had carved out. I felt him like an echo or a musical vibration, a sound that can only arise out of emptiness. Suddenly, I was aware of the bony structures of my body—my cranium, my rib cage, my pelvis—the way they hold or contain me, yet create room for something else—something as ephemeral as spirit or the in-dwelling of life. This kind of emptiness feels different from mere deprivation or the condition of fear that I (like Lewis) associate with loss.

"Sorrow," Lewis writes, "turns out to be not a state but a process. It needs not a map but a history, and if I don't stop writing that history at some quite arbitrary point, there's no reason why I should ever stop." We don't get over grief, I think, but we may learn to live with it—literally, as if grief were a person, disturbingly unmaterial, whom we adjust to on a daily basis, with all the mundane compromises involved in dealing with a real, human being. The dead are not static. They keep changing, just like us, and the conversation is ongoing. We don't stop talking to someone in our heads, just because they have left the room. In this sense, talking with the dead is like praying, or talking with God.

Over time, Lewis came to think of Joy not so much as "present" as somehow available. In *A Grief Observed,* he describes a fleeting "impression of her *mind* momentarily facing my own." There was no message, per se, just a perception of "intelligence and attention. No sense of joy or sorrow. No love even, in our ordinary sense," but "an extreme and cheerful intimacy." One could hardly call this a belief in heaven or even an afterlife, yet it is not nothing.

Can a feeling of nothing be nevertheless something? I want to think so. Recently, I discovered a quirk of English etymology that I find oddly soothing. According to the *Oxford English Dictionary,* the meaning of the word "sad" as sorrowful is relatively modern. At its root—in Old English, Old and Middle High German, Old Teutonic, and Windogermanic, it means "full" or "satisfied." Even the later Latin form means "enough." For the Middle English poet Chaucer, "blysfulnesse" could also be "sad," that is to say "stydefast and parfyt." Slowly, however, "sad" began a journey of its own, from meaning "sated," "strong," "trustworthy," and "valiant," to "grave," "serious," and, at long last, "mournful." I want to turn this around and say that sadness, at some times and in some conditions, may be perceived as satisfying—if not blissful, then at least serious and grave, if not perfect or full, then at least enough.

From the Center:

Blue

whatever
returns from oblivion returns
to find a voice

from the center of my life came
a great fountain, deep blue
shadows on azure seawater.

— Louise Glück, "The Wild Iris"

WHEN I SAW KRZYSZTOV KIEŚLOWSKI'S *Blue*
for the first time, my second marriage, which I had thought
of as stable and enduring, had snapped as sharply as a twig.
The affair that precipitated this rupture had also ended. I
was now alone, with no buffer against the rawness of my
experience—or of my long-ago history. What I saw onscreen,
as a result, had an unusual degree of immediacy. Although
the heroine Julie's trauma was different from mine, I understood her motivation in turning her back on her past. She
was doing exactly what I had tried, and failed, to do—with
similar consequences; she loses the most vital, creative part
of herself. In seeking to evacuate her history, Julie becomes
no one, a person with no feeling or meaning in her life. Recovery from such a state of internal deadness asks that she
embrace the parts of her life she most wants to dismiss. It
also asks her to cry. When, at long last, she arrives at this
moment, she finds a new form of selfhood—one that allows
her to imagine a future.

In the less than three hours it took me to view this film, I could see my journey whole. Julie's path from numbness to mourning paralleled my own glacially slow progress through grief. When I cried this time, I understood why.

Julie's story begins with a car crash that takes the lives of her composer husband and seven-year-old daughter. A series of isolated images portrays this event—a single blue-black tire, viewed from the roadbed, speeding down an asphalt blue highway—shining blue foil, turned this way and that outside the car window—a child resting her arms on the rear window ledge, gazing into the bluish dusk—a youth by the side of the road, playing a game with a wooden ball and cup—the front of the car crumpled against a tree—a beach ball rolling slowly away from the sprung rear door.

We do not see Julie in this sequence. We know that she has survived by the flutter of a feather on her pillow and the reflection of a man in the pupil of her eye. She is breathing and she is conscious. Her first action on learning the news of the death of her husband Patrice and her daughter Anna is to turn her face into the pillow—as if to stifle this information or to negate her own accidental existence. Later, when she is more fully recovered, she makes a deliberate attempt on her life.

Smashing a window to distract the nurse attendant, Julie enters the hospital pharmacy, locates a bottle of pills and pours them into her mouth. After a moment of indecision, she spits them out again, confessing to the nurse "Je ne peux pas. Je ne suis pas capable." (I can't. I'm not able). Although Julie cannot commit suicide, she is not making an active choice for life. Yet this moment of confrontation with death is critical, the point from which Julie's fate begins to unfold and take shape. We do not know what she was like before; her life begins here.

Although I had a life before my father died—one in which I even felt happy—I had no access to it. It seemed unreal, a phantom history, which receded before me each time I approached. As a child, I felt this change without having any way to combat it. My life, which had been malleable up until this point, hardened into a shape I hadn't chosen and which I felt powerless to alter. I not only lost my father, I lost much of my early history—or the use I might have made of it in growing up.

Before the age of seven, when I first became ill with rheumatic fever, I felt comfortable in my body, my family, my neighborhood. I had a best girlfriend who lived across the street from me, a boy I had a crush on who lived down the block, a teacher who favored me in school, and parents whose love and protection I took easily for granted—much as I believed in a personal guardian angel. I can remember the feeling of waking on a summer morning, giddy with the prospect of the day ahead. I'd slip into my T-shirt, sandals, and shorts, gulp down my cereal and orange juice, and rush outside to see who was ready to play. If I saw my best friend, we might do girl things—jump rope, hopscotch, dress up, or some form of make-believe with our dolls. If there was a mix of boys and girls, we played games like tag, Cowboys and Indians, or King of the Mountain. In the sweltering afternoons, we would put on bathing suits and spray each other with the garden hose or run through the sprinklers on our front lawns. In the evenings, we would stay outside as long as possible, playing hide-and-seek or catching fireflies until our mothers called us home.

I have a picture of myself from that time. I'm urging myself forward on our backyard swing, my legs stretched out in front. I've got bangs and short braids and am grinning widely, revealing a missing front tooth. I look like a child who has no self-consciousness, who is so blended into her

world that she trusts it implicitly. If she appears to have no
defenses, it is because she has no need of them.

Being ill and confined to bed with rheumatic fever separated me from my friends and caused me to turn inward, but
it did not shake my confidence in my world. The rhythm of
being sick and then well was something I disliked, but I
could adjust to it. In our family home movies from this period, I move carefully, shyly, but there is no guardedness in
my expression, no shadow across my eyes.

I can see a marked change in a picture of me and my two
brothers taken the first Christmas after my dad's death. We
have been posed with the children of one of my mother's
friends, from whom we stand apart in our solemnity. None of
us is smiling, having ignored the ritual instruction to "say
cheese." I'm a little plump from my most recent bout with
rheumatic fever, my hair long and wavy. I'm wearing a white
fur hat that I had wished for and gotten from Santa. But there
is no sign of pleasure in my face. My expression is wary, my
eyes unreadable. I'm a different girl now.

Not being able to kill herself, Julie tries to jettison her past,
by divesting herself of her personal property, disposing of
the score of unfinished music her husband was working on
at the time of his death, and taking up residence in a quarter
of Paris where she can lose her former identity. In the city,
she is anonymous, a woman with no past and no emotional
ties. After seducing Olivier, her husband's former assistant,
she leaves him, saying that now he knows she is a woman like
any other and that he will not miss her. When she asks Marie,
a faithful family servant, why she is crying, Marie replies,
"Parce que vous ne pleurez pas" (Because you're not).

Julie not only does not cry, she makes a conscious effort
to interrupt the expression of any emotion. If she is awake,
she closes her eyes. If asleep, she wakes up with a start.

Leaving her home and the man she has callously slept with, she scrapes her knuckles against a stone wall. She tries not to see, to feel, to breathe even. She does not break down or break open. Julie is on a campaign to prevent unwanted feelings from arising, to nullify her former life. This is as close to suicide as she can get.

Everything in Julie's behavior made sense to me. Her inability to cry doesn't mean that she's unfeeling; it means that she's feeling too much. Witnessing Julie's desperate attempt to escape her past helped me to understand the way I grew up—amputating pieces of myself as a way of avoiding a head-on confrontation with grief. Like Julie, I had a lot in my life that I wanted to forget. My anguish and terror at my father's death; my resentment of my mother's grief-stricken state of distraction; my hatred of my stepfather; my incestuous attraction to my older brother. By the time I was old enough to leave home, all I wanted was to flee this legacy. My dearest wish was to be released from my history and to be allowed to start over, to reinvent myself. How could I have understood that the resources I needed for such a task were precisely the ones I had given up?

Julie, who signs over her income, changes her name, trashes her husband's musical score, and moves into an apartment building where there are no children to remind her of her dead daughter, nevertheless holds onto some remnants of her past. She removes two things from her country-house estate: a scrap of paper with notes for the conclusion of the symphony her husband was composing at the time of his death and a blue crystal chandelier. Both are "mementos"— the chandelier of some nameless, yet evocative mood, perhaps from childhood, and the notes a reminder of a piece of music by the composer Van den Budenmayer.

In the course of the film, these two survivals from Julie's past fuse into a single, powerful stimulus, recalling her to an awareness not only of her traumatic loss, but also of her suppressed creativity. While the chandelier, which she takes from the music room of her country house, offers a visual representation of the music in her head, the requiem-like refrain of Van den Budenmayer's score alludes to the grief she is trying to negate. Each resurgence of this music challenges Julie not only to remember—and mourn—her loss, but also to acknowledge her part in composing the music attributed to her famous husband.

I, too, salvaged one or two things from my past, carrying them in memory like talismanic objects. My conversation with Jay Landesman in London at my friend Helen's flat recalled one of these—the crystal chandelier that I associated with my father's sensibility and the carefree period of my childhood. Certain landscapes, mostly involving lakes, rivers, or streams, evoked more conflicted responses, reminding me not only of our family outings on the river, but also their tragic conclusion. My love of literature, which I tended to think of as neutral and hence safe, formed a more accessible connection, though one that it took me years to understand. My father, too, had loved books, his library filled with leather-bound editions of Euripides, Cervantes, Molière, Hugo, Tolstoy, Dickens, and Shakespeare. When I first read *Hamlet* in high school, I didn't buy the text ordered for the class. Instead, I went to the living room and pulled out one of my father's dusty volumes.

While suppressing my most painful memories, I maintained enough links with my earlier life to preserve the possibility of recovering them at some future point. I could see Julie doing something similar. While consciously denying her past, she takes steps that permit its resurgence—along with her disavowed talent as a composer.

Mourning, in *Blue,* is related to creativity, an odd, or at least paradoxical, conjunction. Yet not so surprising if we look at mourning as a process that involves the whole of our emotional range—a kind of physical workout that exercises every muscle group of the feelings. A program of total emotional fitness, so to speak. But who, given a choice, wants to feel bad? The dark—the shadow time—of mourning is one that, to my knowledge, no one actively seeks. From the depths of my childhood experience, I understood Julie's seeming heartlessness. If she keeps her gaze focused straight ahead it's out of fear of looking back. Bit by bit, however, Julie's music, the signifier of both her creativity and her loss, claims her.

We first hear the dirge-like strains of Patrice's unfinished symphony during his televised state funeral. Watching from her hospital bed, Julie feels an impulse to cry, but stops herself by squeezing her eyes shut. Later, as she convalesces on the balcony of her room, the music startles her awake. When a woman appears to interview her for a TV retrospective on her husband's career, she asserts that the score for his symphony "n'existe pas." Like her emptied-out life, it is nothing, nowhere. "Is it true," the interviewer persists, "that you composed your husband's music?" Julie turns her back and departs.

Each time the music intrudes into her consciousness, Julie cuts it off. When she starts to pick out a refrain on the piano in her country house, she stops abruptly and slams down the lid. Removing the unfinished score from storage, she can't help hearing the chorus, as the shop assistant moves her finger across the page, praising its beauty. Julie feeds the score to a garbage truck the moment she steps out of the building.

While the music is inside Julie and emerges unbidden, it is also outside of her, a part of her milieu. The first time we see her in a coffee shop, we also hear a strain of music from the street that is so like the music Julie has tried to banish that we begin to wonder if it has actually been stolen. The light on Julie's coffee cup slowly fades and then brightens—a near blackout moment. We next see her swimming furiously across an Olympic-size pool.

The pool is an ambiguous environment. It is silky, enticing, aqueous, a seeming refuge from the sights and sounds that assail Julie from within and without. But it is also shining, like the crystal chandelier; it is liquid, like the tears Julie refuses to shed; and it is blue. Julie flings herself into the very medium she is fleeing, as if to defeat it or to prove her own survival. There are four swimming-pool scenes, each representing a stage in Julie's capitulation to grief. She fights this awareness, paradoxically immersing herself more fully each time in the element that she resists.

My first attempt to keep a journal, the place where I might begin to explore my inner life, was a disaster. It was a small book with a blue cloth cover, given to me by a well-meaning friend. I made only one entry in this book—a brief exchange between two characters in *Twelfth Night*, one of Shakespeare's more convoluted romantic comedies. At the top of the first page, I wrote: "And what's her history?" Immediately underneath, I added: "A blank, my lord."

Viola, who speaks the second line, is in love with the Duke of Orsino, yet unable to reveal her passion, since she is disguised as a boy. She tries to give voice to her feelings by telling a story. "My father had a daughter lov'd a man," she says, "as it might be perhaps, were I a woman/ I would your lordship." "And what's her history?" the Duke asks innocently.

I inscribed this exchange in my journal, then closed the book. When I first looked inside myself, I found no story—not even any words of my own. I felt that I had nothing to say.

Perhaps I identified with Viola because of the complexity of her situation. She arrives on the shores of the Duke's kingdom due to a shipwreck, which separates her from her brother, whom she believes to have drowned. Her disguise, which is meant to protect her in an unfamiliar environment, also serves to mask her state of mourning. Her first words convey her pain and bewilderment. "And what should I do in Illyria?" she says. "My brother he is in Elysium."

I could have said something similar for myself. My life made no sense to me. Without my father, I not only had difficulty charting a future, I also had no idea who I was. Because my history was indecipherable, it might as well have been a blank.

Like Viola, I felt tongue-tied. Even in disguise, however, she finds a way to give expression to some of her feelings, including the awkwardness of her dilemma in relation to the Duke. Speaking obliquely, she describes how stifled she feels by her masculine role. Her father's daughter, she says,

> . . . never told her love,
> But let concealment like a worm i' th' bud
> Feed on her damask cheek; she pin'd in thought,
> And with a green and yellow melancholy,
> She sat like Patience on a monument,
> Smiling at grief.

I, too, was pining in thought. I, too, felt consumed from within. In my fruitless effort to conceal my grief—even to myself—I was turning into some kind of tombstone figure. A monument to suppressed mourning.

Yet, even if my words were borrowed, I had begun to write. Through an adopted persona, I had stated a truth about how I felt. A truth so terrible that I could not bear to confront it. Instead, I shut my new journal and put it away on a shelf. A full year passed before I was ready to try again.

Julie's swimming is like Viola's disguise and my first journal entry—an evasive maneuver. When life begins to claim her, reminding her of her loss, she swims. The second swimming scene occurs after her encounter with Antoine, the young man who witnesses the car crash. The first on the scene after the accident, he discovers a gold chain and cross, which he tries to return to her. She refuses the gift, saying, "Vous l'avez rentrée. C'est à vous." (You have tried to return it. It's yours). During this scene, Julie experiences another black-out, accompanied by the unwanted music. Immediately afterward, she swims, as if to erase this experience. When she hoists herself up out of the water, however, she re-encounters the music. Slowly, she lowers herself back down into the pool and hunches over, her head down, her knees pulled up to her chest in a fetus-like position.

Eventually, I began a new journal—one that I bought for myself. It was big (like an artist's notebook), plain-covered, and black. I purchased a fountain pen in order to write in it. After a couple of pages, however, my ink ran out, which provided enough of an incentive to stop. Once again, I waited almost a year to make a new start.

Gradually, the life in Julie's apartment building begins to claim her. Her refusal to sign a petition condemning the morals of her downstairs neighbor Lucille elicits a thank-you visit from this woman, who makes a living performing sex acts in a nightclub. Julie cannot escape human encoun-

ters or attachments any more than she can eliminate re-
minders of her past. Perhaps the most vivid demonstration
of the intrusiveness of life occurs when she discovers a mouse
and its babies in her pantry closet. The baby mice are tiny,
mewling, and naked. Julie recoils in horror; rodent babies
terrify her.

She then tries to find a new apartment. When this move
fails, Julie pays a visit to her senescent mother in her nursing
home. In a tour de force of noncommunicative dialogue, Julie
presents herself to her mother, who calls her "Marie-France,"
the name of her long-dead sister, marveling that she is still
alive and informing her that Marie-France was not afraid
of mice as a child. "C'est Julie qui avait peur," she comments
accurately, yet disjunctively, her eyes drifting to the TV
screen, where an elderly man makes an improbable bungee
jump toward a distant pool of water. Julie, who has had to
inform her mother that she is not her mother's dead sister,
that she has no home, and that her husband and daughter
are dead, observes dryly that now she is afraid. "Maintenant,
j'ai peur," she says, as if recognizing for the first time how
she actually feels.

So far, Julie's trajectory of grief follows a familiar path.
She wants to deny reality; she wants to die. Failing that, she
wants to obliterate her former identity, to "forget" her past.
Only now does she acknowledge that the emotional world
she inhabits is genuinely frightening and out of her control.

When I took up my journal for a third time, I wrote about
anxiety. My husband and daughter were away on a trip,
leaving me alone for the first time in years. It was spring
break, and I was grading papers. When I wasn't focused on
this task, I didn't know what to do with myself. I ran er-
rands, phoned friends, watched TV, tried to read. I needed
distraction. I was afraid.

Writing—even the little I could do—helped. This time, when my ink ran out, I refilled my pen. I had made a decision of sorts. My history no longer felt like a blank. On the contrary, it was overwhelming. Suddenly there was too much to say, too much to write. I could only record bits and pieces at one sitting. But this time I didn't stop.

Acting on her fear, Julie makes a choice that frightens her even more. She borrows an unneutered cat from a friend and releases it into her apartment to destroy the baby mice. Then she swims.

When Julie surfaces at the far side of the pool, she encounters Lucille, the woman whose behavior has aroused such a storm of protest in her apartment building. Noticing that Julie is crying, she inquires, "Tu pleures?" It's just the water, Julie protests, "C'est l'eau." Lucille offers to clean up after the cat. As she leaves, a group of five- or six-year-old girls in pink water wings rushes past her, plunging into the water. As if remembering her own dead daughter, Julie bows her head, pressing her forehead against the side of the pool.

Lucille, who assumes some of the burden of Julie's pain through her simple act of kindness and words of exoneration ("c'est normal") is also the unwitting agent of her reattachment to life. Sometime later, Julie is awakened in the middle of the night by a phone call from Lucille, who asks Julie to come to her immediately. When she arrives at Lucille's workplace, she learns that Lucille had spotted her father in the audience earlier in the evening and feared that he would stay long enough for her act. By the time Julie appears, however, the crisis has passed; he has already departed. Their attention is then diverted to the stage area, which they view through the window in Lucille's dressing room. Suddenly, Lucille exclaims, "c'est toi là?" And for a moment, as the

camera scans the stage area, we can only assume that Lucille
is identifying Julie with one of the sex performers. When
Julie says yes, "c'est moi," we wonder if she has seen her
uncanny double.

Slowly, in my journal, I began to recognize and recover the
self I had lost. But I held her at arm's length. Turning her this
way and that, examining her like some exotic creature, some
new species of flora or fauna. I scrutinized her with studious
intensity, like a radiologist poring over the phosphorescent
glow of an X ray. I had an obsessive curiosity about what was
inside this girl, this woman. She was definitely interesting to
me, though strange.

When I re-read passages from these journals I am sad-
dened and dismayed. How slow, how dogged, how repetitive
they are. What was I so afraid of? Why couldn't I just inhabit
myself?

When Julie says, "c'est moi," something changes. Through
the window separating Lucille's dressing room from the performance area, we see a TV screen, where Olivier is being
interviewed by the female talk-show host that Julie has
spurned earlier. Not only do we learn that Olivier is working
on Patrice's supposedly nonexistent score, but that there was
another woman in Patrice's life. Both Lucille's exclamation
and Julie's recognition of her own image derive from photographs displayed on the TV, which include snapshots of this
second, background woman. Julie's sudden, unwilled confrontation with her past alters her understanding.

For the first time, she runs. Exiting the music shop, where
she learns that the proprietor kept a copy of the unfinished
symphony, she spies Olivier's car at the end of the street. She
races after it, yelling. When Olivier stops to allow an ambulance to pass, she beats her fists against the rear window to

get his attention. The TV show, Olivier admits, was designed to arouse her from apathy, to make her run, to make her cry ("pour vous faire courir, pour vous faire pleurer").

I once had a romantic interlude with someone who later became a friend. Looking back on our single experience of intense connection, this man mused, "At least I had an impact on you. In the space of four days, I made you angry, and I made you cry."

It was true. Something about this man had cut through my defenses, exposing more feeling than I knew I had at the time. A year or so later, I found myself in a more committed relationship, where I began to reflect on what my friend had said. What had been true earlier was even more true now. As soon as I let down my guard, a geyser of feeling burst forth. The deeper the intimacy, the more volatile I became. While unsettling, this process intrigued me. Instead of shutting down, I opened myself more. Until I reached a turning-point awareness.

I was making love with a degree of abandon I had rarely experienced when suddenly my partner and I both started to come. I could feel my body as continuous with his, as though we were a single organism, a single protoplasm—like some primitive one-celled creature that had not yet learned to differentiate. For a moment, it felt as if there might be no end to this sensation. As if I could stay there forever, in a state of ecstatic, almost mystical, union. I felt deeply integrated, as though I were both intensely and uniquely myself, yet also someone else. I understood, for the first time, what it might mean to merge with another—to be one body, one flesh. Finally, I had to break off. I was too shaken, too flooded with feeling.

I felt overwhelmed and wanted to sleep. When I woke up, I started to cry. My tears flowed gently at first, and then in great racking and wrenching sobs. Now my sorrow felt as endless as my previous state of bliss. It was as though every emotion I had ever felt was located in my pelvis and radiated outward from this core.

My partner was distressed; he didn't understand how such obvious pleasure could lead to such an expression of grief. I didn't blame him, but I couldn't explain myself. All I could do was surrender. Something about this experience felt familiar—the involuntary muscular response that signaled the most intimate feeling of fusion, swiftly followed by the most devastating feeling of loss.

Finally, I understood.

Intimacy itself lay at the heart of my dilemma. It was love that had hurt me and love that I avoided—until I could no longer bear my isolation. Yet each time I formed a close attachment, I became anxious, anticipating a repetition of my childhood abandonment. Love was my enemy. I feared it would destroy me.

Once Julie stops resisting her fate, her life takes a new course. From this moment forward, her choices assist this process. First, she accepts Olivier's offer to listen to his additions to Patrice's score. In the midst of this encounter, she reminds him that the words to the final chorus are drawn from the New Testament—the rhythm of which (in Greek) he has not captured. Next, she asks about Patrice's lover. On learning her identity, Julie experiences another music-filled blackout. Then she decides to find her and confront her in person.

Julie's meeting with Sandrine, a lawyer who works for a judge, reveals a dimension of her life that she had been ignorant of. Her husband not only loved his mistress—she wears the same gold chain and cross that Julie had—but he has left her pregnant. Following this encounter, Julie swims for one last time. We hear her plunge into the water, but do not see her until she bursts forth, gasping for air at the far end of the pool. Diving deep, swimming underwater, and holding her breath will not protect her from what she now knows. Or from what she feels.

The only way I know to recover from traumatic loss is to feel it. Not only to have the emotions associated with the loss but to connect them to their source. Merely repeating the experience in a milder, disguised form does not relieve the underlying distress. While it may serve to let off steam, it does not heal the heart's catastrophe.

Yet to a fragile psyche, annihilation feels a more likely possibility than release. It's too much like dying—with no hope of an afterlife. When Julie smashes the hospital window, she conveys how she feels within. She is splintered, disintegrated.

For many years, when I cried at the movies I was crying for myself, yet unable to make the most obvious connection between what I saw on the screen and painful events in my own life. Then, one weekend, on a visit to the Basilica of the Immaculate Conception in Washington, D.C., I suddenly started to cry for my own history of loss.

I was on a business trip, attending a conference on Shakespeare over the Easter weekend. On Saturday, I had some free time and decided to explore the Basilica, which bore the name of the neighborhood parish church I had attended as a child. As a national shrine, the Basilica is something of a sight-seeing attraction, so I signed up for the guided tour. When it was over, I decided to sit in the church by myself—for a moment of solitude and reflection.

In this peaceful atmosphere, I started to think about my family and my father in particular, reliving the moments preceding his disappearance. I remembered how he had been

angry with me and my two brothers the day he died, then
how his mood relaxed. How he had asked me to wash his
back as we camped on the beach and how happy I was to do
this. How I worked up a lather, then splashed a bucket of
river water over him to wash the soap off. How relieved I was
that he was no longer angry. How heartily he laughed.

Then he was gone.

This time, when I started to cry, I knew what I was crying
about. I'm not sure how long I sat there, alternately letting my tears flow and swiping at them with Kleenex. There
weren't many people in the corner area where I sat, but I
didn't care what they thought. What better, what safer place
to cry than a church?

Gradually, my thoughts began to shift to my stepfather. I
pictured his loneliness as a child, his own bereavement. It
was clear to me that he had married my mother in order to
have a family. He had done nothing to hurt me. His only fault
was his own sadness. How could I blame him for that? I
wished that he had not died in the way that he did—with no
one to help him. I wished he were still alive so I could ask his
forgiveness.

I cried in waves—remembering, regretting, feeling sad,
and wishing I could make up for everything that had gone
awry in my family. My grief was heartfelt and deep. I had
never felt so sorry.

Finally, my tears subsided. I got up and walked out into
the mild spring air. The sky had been sunny when I arrived,
but a flash storm had occurred while I was inside, leaving
shining pools of water on the stone steps. How appropriate, I
thought, to Holy Saturday, the day of gnashing of teeth and
tearing of hair. The day of requiem, the day of mourning.

Once Julie chooses to confront her past—by meeting
Sandrine—she no longer resists the music in her head. She

returns to Olivier and asks to see his symphonic notes. Then she begins giving instructions, assuming personal responsibility for completing the score that she may have had a hand in composing while her husband was alive.

Julie pens the last notes, a flute solo reminiscent of the Van den Budenmayer fragment she saved from the music room, and then calls Olivier. Her last words to him, "Je viens" (I'm coming), echo her call to Anna—the first words spoken in the film, seconds before the crash. From this point forward, the music unfolds without interruption, as the camera performs a continuous pan, connecting the fates of the main characters: Olivier and Julie, Antoine, Julie's mother, Lucille, Sandrine and her unborn child. Coming full circle, the camera returns to Julie, seated with her back to Olivier, her chin resting lightly on her clasped hands as she gazes directly into the camera, tears flowing silently down her cheeks.

Julie isn't convulsed by her sorrow. Rather, she seems accepting of it. Her tears—the evidence of her acknowledgment of her loss—permit release. It wasn't until the Easter weekend in Washington that I realized how much I had been hedging the finality of my father's departure. Only then did I understand how much I associated the manner of his death with the ritual of Holy Week. I believed he had died on a Friday and that his body was found the following Sunday. Once, I came across a letter from a priest to my older brother in the immediate aftermath of my dad's death. This well-meaning man tries to console my brother by likening my father's choice to go to his rescue to the sacrifice of Christ. "There is no greater love than this," he reminds my brother, not even beginning to imagine the possibility that such a message might leave my brother intolerably burdened with guilt. While I did not share this legacy as a child, there was no question in my own, heavily Catholicized mind that my father was some kind of savior—yet one who failed to rise from the dead.

It wasn't until after my mother died that I finally got the sequence straight. August 30, 1951, fell not on a Friday but a Thursday, which meant that my father's body was discovered the following Saturday—not Sunday, as I had always thought. Forty-seven years after my father's death, this comprehension came as a shock. I didn't realize until then how much I had mythologized his departure, how implicitly I relied on his return. My daddy was not God; he wasn't coming back.

What Julie learns from her husband's mistress is that her marriage was not as wonderful as she had thought. The happiness she remembers—and tries to enshrine by hermetically sealing the past—was not perfect. This realization of imperfect love releases her into her present life, into the love she can offer and that is offered to her, as well as her capacity for creative expression.

Julie, who has resisted the motion of time, which has altered her life so irreparably, finally succumbs to it, as she succumbs to the pressure of her grief. Her decision to bequeath her husband's name and his estate to Sandrine and her unborn child represents a letting go of her former life, including the simple happiness it seemed to embody. In place of her lost maternity (images of which she has desperately tried to evade), she embraces her artistic talent. Accepting the pain of her deprivation is synonymous with accepting the music in her head. A real, if ghostly, consolation.

The unfolding of the full musical score begins as Julie touches the final note she has penned and continues, uninterrupted, through the film's final credits. The chorus enters as the camera moves from a close-up to a long shot in Julie's apartment, revealing the blue chandelier suspended over her worktable. From this point, the camera movement is continuous, though locations and individuals are separated by black screens, which act like beats of music, rather than full stops.

The unfolding of my inner life, including my discovery of a creative self, was not so smooth. When I started to write something other than journal entries, the feelings I gave voice to were often despairing. One early poem, in particular, comes to mind. In it, I tried to say something about the deadness I felt within and my fear that it would never go away. I wrote:

> We can't make it better.
> The seaweed, the rotting fish
> we drag up won't be prettier
> in the living room dried
> or pried loose from its flesh.
> The smooth bone will stink
> whatever we do to it, here
> or on the beach.

I was thinking of Ariel's song from *The Tempest*, sung for the benefit of Ferdinand, who believes his father has drowned in the storm that has shipwrecked him on Prospero's magic island. Ariel's song hints not only at consolation, but at transfiguration.

> Full fadom five thy father lies,
> Of his bones are coral made:
> Those are pearls that were his eyes:
> Nothing of him that doth fade,
> But doth suffer a sea-change
> Into something rich and strange.

The Tempest, like *Twelfth Night*, had always had resonance for me, because of the way it begins with drowning and shipwreck. Whereas consolation is easy in these plays, in which death turns out not to be real—both Viola's brother and Ferdinand's father show up alive and well—in my own life I could find no such relief. My poem continues:

> Eyes will never turn to pearls.
> Coral can't be made from bone.
> Words, like everything else,
> decompose.

To undergo the kind of sea-change evoked by Ariel's song, I felt that I would need something like a heart transplant.

Julie's transformation not only releases the storehouse of her music and the wellspring of her tears, it also opens her heart. The words for the chorus (sung in Greek), which we hear only fully in the last sequence of the film, are taken from St. Paul's first letter to the Corinthians. As rendered in my English sub-titled version, they read:

> Though I speak with the tongues of angels
> If I have not love
> I am become as hollow brass
>
> Though I have the gift of prophecy
> And understand all mysteries
> And all knowledge
> And though I have enough faith
>
> To move the mightiest mountains
> If I have not love
> I am nothing
> Love is patient
> Love is kind
>
> Love never fails

For prophecies shall fail
Tongues shall cease
Knowledge shall wither away

Knowledge shall wither away

And now shall abide

Faith, hope, and love

But the greatest of these
Is love

This message of love not only makes sense of Julie's return to Olivier and their literal lovemaking, but it also suggests a way to view the final sequence of images linking the fates of the central characters. There is no dialogue from the moment that Julie touches her finger to the score until the end of the film. The only words are those sung by the chorus.

First we see a hand on Julie's shoulder. Her face is pressed against glass, presumably a window. Olivier is making love to her from behind. As the camera moves upward, we see some kind of dense foliage at the top of the window, rendering the whole scene enigmatic—as if the lovers were underground or underwater. The blue light reminds us of the swimming pool. It is as if we are looking at Julie and Olivier through the glass of an aquarium.

Next, we view a hand move to a clock to stop an alarm. Antoine, waking into a blue-lit room, fingers the gold cross and chain he wears around his neck. From Antoine's room, we move to the reflection of Julie's mother's face in a window. The camera shifts to another reflection of her face, this time in profile, then to a frontal view, as she slowly closes her eyes. Through the patio door, we see a nurse running up the steps.

From the nursing home, we move into the sex club where Lucille works. The camera lingers on two female figures in the middle of a performance, then on Lucille's face in half shadow. After this red-lit space, we move into the greenish light of a doctor's office, where a hand rests on Sandrine's belly, applying an ultrasound device. The camera pauses on the ultrasound screen, where we view a full image of the baby in Sandrine's womb. Sandrine's face appears, framed by two ultrasound screens—one evidently a reflection.

As the choral music subsides, the camera returns to Olivier and Julie, focusing on the image of Julie's back reflected in the pupil of Olivier's eyes. There is a reprise of the requiem-like music from the beginning of the film. Julie sits on the edge of the bed, her hands clasped lightly in front of her chin, as tears flow down the left side of her face. Slowly, reflections begin to appear in the windowpane that separates her from the camera—and our viewing. We see the swaying shadow of a tree, as a bluish light plays across the glass. Julie's tears are now flowing freely. Finally, she lowers her eyes. The music continues through the credits, coming to rest with Julie's flute solo—then four, isolated pulse notes, not unlike a heartbeat.

Like Julie, I have tried to cut my emotional losses by severing my ties with my past. It was a devil's bargain that I made. In turning my back on grief, I gave up the hope of future solace, including the blessings and possibilities of love.

"It is terrible to survive," as Louise Glück says in her poem "The Wild Iris," "as consciousness buried in the dark earth," and surely suppressed grief feels like this. Like inhabiting a tomb of one's own making. How could I have foreseen that the emotion I most resisted—crying—would remove the stone from this crypt? That water, for me the very medium of loss, would also serve as a means of release?

Until recently, I have been unable to think such a thought, but I was able to imagine it once—in a dream.

I am standing on a cliff overlooking the ocean. Looking down, I see that people are being killed on the beach below. Suddenly, I think of a way to rescue *one* of them, but in order to do this I have to impersonate Death—by putting on a dark costume with a black, birdlike mask. I descend from the cliff and enter the water, where I am partly buoyed up and partly weighed down by my voluminous cloak. I lie on my back, kicking away from the shore, trying to catch a current that will bear me out to sea, where I can slip free of my disguise, undetected.

This dream frightened me at first. It seemed sinister. Who wants to be Death? The image of myself floating on the water with my cloak billowing around me also reminded me of Shakespeare's Ophelia—not to my mind an auspicious association. Ophelia, in *Hamlet,* dies a quasi-suicide, drifting for a while "mermaid-like" on the currents of water into which she falls before her waterlogged clothes drag her down. Yet my father had told my brother Bob to "float" (which he knew how to do), to ease his panic about being in water over his head. To this day, my brother believes that my dad's advice is what saved him from drowning. I also remember my mother telling us kids, as we piloted our boat away from the sandbar to seek help, that my dad might still be alive if he drifted downriver and found a buoy to cling to. So, in this dream, I float. I may be Ophelia, but I am not drowning.

I'm swimming out to sea, where I plan to give Death the slip. Only in an element as fluid and changeable as water can I perform such a feat.

I have always loved being near water. Fountain, stream, river, lake, or sea—it doesn't matter which. Water moves and catches light. You can't capture or contain it. It slips through your hands, but will allow you to immerse yourself. It can hold or embrace you—or sweep you away.

I know that my father's body was found, placed in a casket, and buried. But I used to think of him as floating down the Mississippi all the way to the Gulf of Mexico, where he would have entered and merged with the ocean. It's a piece of fancy, a metaphor of sorts, but I still find it consoling.

Pisces, my astrological sign—which I used to hate, like the fish I was forced to eat on Friday as a child—now seems appropriate. Water is restless, shimmery, elusive, a medium of mutability. Like crying, which also signals a change of state—a sudden liquefaction, transforming dry to wet. We make tears as easily as we metabolize food, our bodies the genies that perform such simple, even daily, tasks. The main ingredient of our seemingly solid selves is water, and we can literally die without it. Even our skin is permeable, exuding and leaking, or in need of hydration.

The lesson of crying is metamorphosis.

Shadow Love
1998

IN CRYING AT THE MOVIES, I have been mourning for myself. For the father I lost, for the child I once was, for everything hopeful in me that felt severed at the moment of his death. But life did not stop for this process. As my grief for my father subsided, other changes were occurring. My mother's health began to go into decline. I was now confronting actual, rather than imagined, orphanhood. Death, you might say, had caught up with me—but in real time, as opposed to traumatized amnesia or fantasy.

So I choose to end this meditation on movies and mourning with an account of my mother's last illness and death. My journey through her final year, while it left many issues between us unresolved, helped me to understand better the life she had lived and my own relation to it. I was experiencing, for the first time, a normal death—in contrast to the way that my father (and stepfather) had departed. The week of my mother's funeral brought this awareness sharply into focus.

After my mother's funeral, I sit on the floor in her bedroom and go through the drawers of her vanity, looking for something—I'm not sure what—a clue to her personality, or maybe just something to hold onto. I lift the pleated skirt that hides the drawers and pull them out, one by one. They are full of oddments: Mother's Day cards made from school construction paper, letters my older brother wrote home from camp, dusty lace-edged handkerchiefs, a broken strand of pearls wrapped in tissue. And photographs. This is where my mother kept her wedding pictures—a handful of black-and-white snapshots—of her marriage to my father in 1938.

One of them, a 3 × 5, is set, slightly off-kilter, in a small gilt frame. When I leave my mother's house in St. Louis to return to my own home in Minneapolis, I take this photo with me.

I also take a postcard and a box of slides—mementos of my parents' life together and its abrupt conclusion when my father drowned thirteen years later.

The postcard, dated November 18, 1950, from Honolulu, Hawaii (where my parents went together on one of my father's business trips), is only slightly larger than their wedding picture. It's a hand-colored photo of Waikiki Lau Yee Chai, "the world's most beautiful Chinese restaurant," a long stucco building with a green tile roof, a pagoda at one end, and pots of red flowers lining the entrance. Addressed to my two brothers and me and written in my mother's sloping hand, it reads:

> *Dear kids,*
> *Daddy and I had dinner at this restaurant and today*
> *Daddy had his hair cut by a Japanese lady barber. Be*
> *good children & Mama will be home soon. Mama*

The box of slides dates from the same trip. Most, I can see from holding them up to the light, are landscape shots, but some show my parents together. These are precious images, since we have so few family photographs that include them both. They make a beautiful couple, both dark-haired and slim, my mother just turned thirty-four, my father a young forty-one. I squint at them, trying to make out what they were feeling at this golden moment of pleasure and success— a mere nine months before my father died. The figures are so small and the lighting so uncertain—an intense blue-green for the most part—that I find it hard to tell.

Real time unfolds in a simple chronological progression. One thing happens, and then another thing, and then something else. It's like the orderly succession of dates and events in a history book. But emotional time has its own logic. Like an unruly current, it follows its own insidious will. When my mother dies, time suddenly compresses. Her death and that of my father have been on a secret collision course for forty-seven years, the time it takes for my mother to join him at the gravesite next to his.

By her early eighties, my mother had a spectrum of ailments: congestive heart failure, emphysema, diabetes, and osteoarthritis—which she managed to control for over a decade through a daily cocktail of diuretics, cardiac meds, and painkillers, spiked with insulin. Then, about a year before she died, things took an abrupt turn for the worse.

In the fall of 1997, I went to St. Louis for Thanksgiving— my "annual duty visit," as my mother put it, not too kindly. We had been edgy with each other in recent years, especially since my second divorce. My mother, who never seemed to approve of my decisions, now saw me as messing up big-time. "Things will not get better," she had warned me ominously when I finally broke the news. "They will only get worse." Her voice, flat and definitive, sent a chill through me, as if she were looking into a crystal ball and reading my fate. After this, I began spacing my calls and visits more widely than before. Yet I kept wishing (and hoping that my mother wished) for something better, for a clearer, warmer, deeper understanding between us. I was hoping for a late-winter thaw in the permafrost of our relationship.

The day I arrived, my mother seemed anxious about coming down with something. She asked my brother Ron to buy her some zinc lozenges, hoping to ward off whatever it was. But the next day, she took to her bed, felled by something too powerful to resist. When she didn't get up except to use her bedside commode, I began to worry. She was not eating, not checking her blood sugar, not taking any of her prescribed medications. Ron and I conferred about this in whispers. My mother had always insisted on doing things her own way. We might plead or cajole, but we knew that we couldn't force her.

On Thanksgiving Day, she was not up to anything. So I cooked the dinner that she had expected to prepare—turkey breast, cranberry sauce, sweet potatoes, salad, green beans, and mincemeat pie—and then asked her to join us at the table. From her makeshift bed in the downstairs sunroom, where she was used to napping in the afternoons, she said no. "I'm not hungry," she insisted in a dull voice. Ron offered to fix her a tray. She was adamant. "You children go ahead and eat your dinner," she said. "I just want to sleep."

Another day without nutrition, another day without the medications she needed to drain the excess fluids from her body, to regulate her blood sugar, to keep her heart pumping in a regular and predictable rhythm. I imagined the constellation of her vital functions beginning to go haywire, like planets slowly spinning out of orbit.

Despite antibiotics, my mother did not seem to improve. She lay in her bed, listless and impassive, refusing everything: food, jokes, conversation. Rebuffed, I pulled back, but my brother Ron was surprisingly cheerful and resilient. When his efforts to tease my mother into eating failed, he brought her chocolate milk shakes, enticing her into taking liquid nourishment. I was torn between anxiety and relief. How long could she go without her other medications? What about her blood sugar, I wondered? What about her heart?

Then she began to have diarrhea, a problem that Ron, who had lived in the same house with her for years, could not deal with. He could empty her commode; he could change and launder the sheets, but he could not provide the personal care my mother needed.

"You're a woman," he said simply. "She needs your help."

I knew he was right, but my heart quailed at the prospect.

My mother and I had never been close. We didn't phone each other on a regular basis. We didn't do "girl talk." When I left home for college at age eighteen, I turned my head resolutely away from St. Louis, knowing that I would never come back there to live. I suppose my mother knew what I was doing—that I was leaving her to her own life.

"You have to clean her," Ron insisted.

My mother had been refusing our joint efforts to get her to eat regular meals, to take her cardiac medications, or to give herself insulin injections. Now I was expected to attend to her most intimate bodily needs. How was I going to do this, I wondered, when I had never even seen her naked?

I took a deep breath and approached the bed, where my mother lay with her eyes closed, covered to the chin with blankets.

"Would you like me to help you wash?" I said.

My mother was silent, as if she hadn't heard me, a tactic she used when she didn't want to engage, but I took it as a positive sign that she didn't resist.

"I'll get some water," I said, not giving her a chance to say no. "It won't take me a minute."

Relieved perhaps, my mother submitted to this entirely new experience of having her gown lifted, being turned in her bed, and having her bottom wiped by her fifty-five year old daughter. Having no words for what I was doing, I tried to focus on the task at hand. Somewhere in the midst of this process—after I had disposed of my mother's soiled underpants—and was wringing the washcloth in the bowl of water I had brought from the kitchen, she commented wryly, "We've come full circle."

I understood what she meant. I could only begin to imagine how painful and humiliating she felt this role reversal to be. "It's only temporary," I said lightly, sensing that it wasn't.

A few months later, I received a phone call from my mother's internist.

"Your mother has three, interrelated problems," she said matter-of-factly. "Sleep apnea, pulmonary hypertension, and a heart arrhythmia. The adjustment of her diuretics is not working too well at this point. They can't be increased without damaging her kidneys, so it's not a realistic goal to get all the fluid off of her lungs. Your mom is pretty sick, and she's getting worse."

That night, I cried long and hard, surprising myself with the strength of my reaction. I was used to a mix of feelings in relation to my mother—longing and frustration, need and resentment, anger and desire. I wanted to please her and make her happy, though nothing I offered or did ever seemed good enough. I wanted her love and approval, though I seemed to incur mostly criticism and disappointment. I wanted something from her that she seemed unable or unwilling to give. No matter how hard I tried, I could not make peace with this painful reality. Instead, I kept wishing and wanting, feeling alternately hopeful and anxious, rebuffed and then hurt. Now, suddenly, I saw her vulnerability. The gravity of her illness cut through my usual snarl of response. Like some ugly mass of hair and sludge, it broke loose from its place of obstruction around my heart, releasing a rush of tenderness and regret.

My anger now felt petty to me—a focus on my own childish need—when we were faced with something bigger. I wanted to be adequate to this challenge, but I didn't have the faintest idea how to change our way of relating to each other. In the end, I did not succeed. My mother's medical problems moved center stage, overwhelming my attempts to forge a new kind of connection. At the same time, something in me did begin to shift. I had glimpses of death as something other than an arbitrary and violent disruption—the way I had experienced my father's abrupt disappearance when I was nine. For the first time in my life, I began to imagine the transition from life to death as taking place on a continuum. Less of an amputation than a transformation. My mother, who was about to leave me, was on the verge of joining my father in the nameless place where his spirit resided. I felt that there was something appropriate about this.

As my mother's eighty-second birthday approached the following fall, I wondered what to give her. Every year, I faced this dilemma. In a material sense, she had everything she could wish for. She had expensive jewelry, clothes, furs. Her house was full of silver, crystal, and antique furniture. She had no use for anything more. In years past, I had tried sending items of comfort, like a down robe or bed covering; technological gadgets, like a portable CD player or speaker telephone; gourmet foods, exotic plants, or beautiful little art objects to add to her collection. One year, in desperation, I sent her a museum reproduction of an Egyptian cat goddess. Nothing seemed to satisfy. Each year, she would thank me for my "thoughtful gift," but I could hear the lack of enthusiasm in her voice. Once again, I had failed to make the right offering; I had failed to please.

Then, one day, I had an inspiration. Earlier in the year, I had had a small snapshot of my parents (taken on the steps of the chapel where they were married) enlarged into an 8 × 10 photograph, intending to keep it for myself. On the spur of the moment, I bought a frame, then packed and mailed this gift before giving myself a chance to reconsider. Often, I procrastinated so long in choosing a present that it arrived late.

This one—even if it turned out to be inappropriate—would get there on time.

I included a card with news, happy birthday wishes, and a message of love, but it was the picture that conveyed what I truly felt. My mother's marriage to my father represented the best time of her life. She had never recovered from his loss. Her persistent unhappiness—which I kept trying and failing to alleviate—flowed from this inexhaustible source. Now that her own life was ending, I thought she might feel less fearful if she could imagine death as less of an ending than a reunion. My parents, who had been separated for over forty-five years, belonged together. This was my own consolation. Picturing them together at last made it just barely tolerable for me to lose them both.

I had no idea what was going through my mother's mind or heart. She was not in the habit of revealing how she felt and her worsening medical condition did not change her disposition. It occurred to me that my present might shock or offend her, that it might violate her sense of propriety by intruding into an area she considered private, even sacrosanct. I waited, with some trepidation, then called on her birthday.

"I received your lovely card," she said, "and your gift." There was an awkward silence, as if she couldn't find a way to acknowledge how different it was from anything I had ever sent before.

"I'm so glad," I said, trying to cover this moment of mutual embarrassment. "I thought about bringing it for Thanksgiving, but wanted you to have it now."

My mother said nothing, so I rushed on, giving her the details of my travel plans for my upcoming visit. Whatever emotion my mother may have been struggling with, she found no words to express. I may even have deprived her of this opportunity by chattering on about my plane reservations.

"I love you," I said, belatedly, as the conversation wound

down. But she was already hanging up. Eight days later, she was dead.

The moment I had been dreading had arrived—sooner than I anticipated. I had been expecting to spend Thanksgiving assessing my mother's most recent medical problems: rectal bleeding and blistered and infected toes. Both my brother Ron and my mother's daytime caregiver had expressed concern about these, and I knew I would have to do something—most likely against my mother's will. She would submit to a doctor's visit only as a last resort. I couldn't help thinking that she had beaten me to the punch. She had managed to die on her own terms—relatively quickly, at home, and without punishing forms of medical intervention.

"She said she wasn't feeling well," Ron told me when I finally reached him. "But she sent me to the grocery store. And she wanted me to check out a new kind of hospital bed, which I did. When I got back, I asked her if she wanted a hamburger and milk shake—which I always bring her on Saturday—but she said no, she still didn't feel good. She went into the sunroom to lie down for a nap. I was sitting there at the breakfast table, eating my burger and sorting my mail, when I looked into the sunroom and noticed her head at a funny angle with her mouth open. Her right arm was also hanging off the bed. So I went in to check on her. I called her and tried to rouse her, but she wouldn't wake up. Then I dialed 911, and they told me how to give mouth-to-mouth resuscitation. I did this until the paramedics came. They took her to the hospital, and I waited in the emergency room for an hour or so. Finally a doctor came out and told me she was gone. He said I could see her, and I went in to say good-bye, but I had to leave her there until we decide on a funeral home."

My brother went over the story several times, saying that

he was worried when my mom said she didn't feel right. "I'm gonna die," she had said once, rather abruptly. But when he offered to call the doctor, she had shouted no.

"You can't blame yourself," I told him. "You and I both know how Mom needed to be in control. You did everything you could; you didn't do anything wrong."

Several times during this conversation I started to cry, and when I hung up I broke down sobbing. My fantasy of being with my mother at the moment of her death was just that—a fantasy. I had done nothing to help her.

Later, I called my older brother and my daughter in New York, made arrangements to miss work at the beginning of the week and to fly to St. Louis the following day. I had no experience in planning a funeral, and neither did Ron. Most of my conversations with him over the years had been about my mother's health. It's as if we had only one subject of interest and one channel of communication. We had never discussed what would happen once she was gone. I figured we were going to have to wing it.

—

When I pull into the driveway in my rental car, I see Ron ahead of me, just getting out of his. I walk over to him and put my arms around him—a gesture that neither he nor I is used to. Typically, we stand awkwardly while saying hello or give each other a quick peck on the cheek. This time there is a real hug.

"I just got back from interviewing a funeral home director," Ron says. "I have another appointment at 5:00. I need to put some things in the house. You can stay here if you want, or you can come with me."

"I'll come with you," I say, pulling a Kleenex from my purse to dry my eyes. "Let me get my bags out of the car first."

Ron and I, who have never cooperated in any serious

endeavor—other than taking my mother to the doctor—are suddenly a team. Never in my wildest dreams have I imagined such a possibility. Yet we move into this uncharted territory with a delicacy of awareness and appreciation of each other's presence that is as surprising as it is gratifying.

Our first task is to choose a funeral home. Ron has already rejected one on the grounds of expense. Mom, he feels sure, would not have wanted us to pay so much. The one we visit together seems more reasonable. As Ron goes over the details of the standard package, I begin to think about my mother's body lying in a cold room somewhere at the hospital. We have to get her out of there as quickly as possible. When the funeral director comes to a pause in his presentation, I ask if he would mind stepping out of the room while Ron and I talk.

"You seem inclined toward this place," I say. "And I think we have to come to a decision soon. It's already Sunday night, and Bob is coming tomorrow evening. If we don't have the funeral by Wednesday, we'll have to wait until after Thanksgiving. We have to get a notice in the paper and arrange for visitation by Tuesday at the latest, so if we can agree on this place now that would help. Then we can go ahead and choose a casket."

Ron agrees, so we sign a contract on the basics and go downstairs with the funeral director to look at caskets. They come in all different colors—pink, gray, steel blue, aqua, maroon, and wood-grain. Some have more lace and frills than others, which I feel sure my mother would not like, her taste running toward simplicity. It doesn't take long for Ron and me to make our choice. Almost wordlessly, we gravitate toward a dark gray model with a smooth white interior and chrome handles. It seems to fit with my mother's character and falls in the mid-range of expense. There are moments when I can't help marveling at our aplomb. What we are doing is so unusual as to border on the surreal, at the same time that it seems entirely natural.

Although improvised, my mother's funeral, in its hour-by-hour and day-by-day unfolding, feels completely appropriate to me. It is like watching an exotic flower that blooms once a century gradually disclose its richness, perfume, and depth. For my whole life, I have dreaded this moment. Not having grieved my father's death, I cannot imagine confronting the loss of my mother. Now that I am actually faced with this reality, I find that it has a dignity, naturalness, and solemnity that astonishes me. There is a spontaneous choreography to the next few days in which every step we take feels new and surprising, yet also simple and right. I begin to observe myself in this process, meeting each moment with little or no preconception of what it might hold, yet feeling its subsequent inevitability.

I am also anxious. I sense my mother's hovering presence, wanting me to do things right. I don't want to disappoint her. In the end, I feel that the funeral Ron and I arrange, though modest, is what she would have wished. Each step along this path, as hazardous as it seems from moment-to-moment, is full of revelation.

After deciding on a funeral home, Ron and I face another set of challenges: composing her obituary, choosing the clothes she will be buried in, and selecting her cemetery plot. Phone calls to area relatives help with the first, but the second is one that undoes me.

I have been sleeping in my mother's bedroom—for reasons I can barely articulate—the most practical of which has to do with the bedside telephone. I can call my friends, long-distance, late at night, and tell them about my day. More buried reasons have to do with my sense of inheritance—of my mother's history, with all its painful ambivalence. I sleep in the bed in which my mother has slept alone for so many years, but this is the same bed in which my stepfather died when I was barely eighteen. Maybe I want, now, to own this complex history. To absorb it, as if by osmosis, through the covers, mattress, and sheets.

On Monday morning, I begin to go through my mother's closet and bureau drawers, looking for something to bury her in. I look for a dress first. Her closet is so full that it is hard to see anything without pulling it out. There are suits that seem dignified enough, but they are all in bright colors. The dresses are too summery, too casual, or too festive. And what about shoes? There must be over fifty pair stacked in Lucite boxes on a shelf. Just then, Ron comes in.

"I don't know what to do," I say. "Nothing seems appropriate, but we're going to have to choose something."

"How about the closet in the guest room," Ron says. "Maybe there's something in there."

The guest room is equally packed. This one has dresses I recognize from earlier times in my mother's life—including the evening dress she wore to my wedding and a designer muumuu from her long-ago trip to Hawaii. Finally, I spy something that might do, a pleated faille skirt and jacket with a muted floral pattern against a dark blue background. My mother will look pretty in this, I think. And it is somber enough for a funeral. Now there is just the matter of accessories.

I go back to the bedroom and search for underthings—bra, panties, slip, stockings. The thought of her naked under her suit and blouse doesn't seem right. But I'm not sure of the size. My mother never threw anything out, so she has lingerie in all proportions—from the time when she was slim in her forties, then increasingly heavy in her fifties, sixties, and seventies, to the present. I don't know which might be the best fit. I hold up first one bra, then another, trying to picture my mother's shrunken breasts fitting into their cups. Ron finds me there, standing in the middle of the room, staring at various combinations of underwear laid out on the bed.

"I just can't," I say, and start to cry. I move toward my brother, who opens his arms and holds me gently, while I try to explain my dilemma. "This is the hardest part," I say, in another rush of tears. "Choosing her clothes makes it all real."

Finally, we are ready to go back to the funeral home, where we hand over my mother's outfit, help to compose an obituary, and confer with the director about the cemetery plot.

"I thought we could handle this by phone," he says, apologetically. "But your family's plot is laid out in a way that makes it hard to interpret. The cemetery had to fax it in sections." He hands us a taped-together piece of paper. "Most plots are rectangular; yours is in pie-shaped wedges," he explains. "It's hard to tell exactly where your mother's grave should be. I'm afraid you're going to have to go out there and talk to them yourself."

I remember, at most, two or three trips to Calvary cemetery, where my mother's near and distant relatives, including my father and stepfather, are buried. Because I was not allowed to attend my father's funeral, I had a special interest in his grave and would sneak glances at it when my mother and I made one of our brief visits. She would talk, on those occasions, about her ancestors, how they died and where they were buried, but not about my father. There was something taboo about this subject, hence my anxiety about looking directly at his gravestone.

We arrive at the gates of the cemetery and drive to the ample Lucas plot, laid out over a century ago by Jean Baptiste Charles Lucas for his family and their many descendants. An obelisk stands in the center, with individual sections radiating outward from it in a pie-shaped design. My mother's site is over a slight hill. As we walk toward it, we can see that a fresh grave has already been dug. But it appears to be in the wrong spot. Instead of lying parallel with that of my father, it is one plot in front.

This makes no sense. Ron and I consult the taped-together piece of paper the funeral director has given us. Based on our reading, the grave is definitely misplaced. We decide to go to the main office to straighten things out.

No one at the front desk seems able to understand what we are talking about. Finally, the foreman, a ruddy, open-faced man in his mid-forties, offers to help.

"At some point in time," he explains, "the grave markers were switched from the head to the foot position. If the first tier of graves starts here, and these are all headstones, then the second ring has to start here, and your mother's and father's graves would be in this ring." He takes a pencil from his shirt pocket and sketches a casket diagram on the fax sheet.

"We're pretty sure this is wrong," Ron says, moving his finger from the casket outline to a spot in the next tier. "We think his grave is here instead."

I am feeling confused. "What if my father's grave marker is a footstone?" I say. "Wouldn't that mean that Ron is right? In any case, a grave has already been dug, and we think it may have to be moved. It would help if you could take a minute and come with us to look at the plot."

"No problem," says the foreman, "I'll get my truck and meet you there."

Comparing the fax sheet with the site, the foreman explains, once again, how they have interpreted the tiers. But there is no way to know for sure where my father's body is buried. It all comes down to whether his marker is a head- or a footstone.

"There's a way we can settle this," the foreman says finally.

"Does your father's grave have a concrete vault? If so, we can put a probe down and find out where it is. I have one in my truck. We can do this right now, if you want."

"Yes," I say, before I have time to think. "Why not get this over with?"

The foreman returns with a harpoon-like object, which he sticks into the ground in the space next to the freshly dug grave. He pumps it down several feet and then a few more without meeting any obstruction.

"Well, he's not here," the foreman says. "Do you want to try this one too, just to be sure?"

This time Ron speaks first. "It isn't necessary," he says. "We already know what we need to know."

Although the river was dragged where my father drowned, his body was not found until it surfaced on its own. By then, it was unrecognizable. My uncle identified him by a cat's-eye sapphire ring he wore. Bloated and gaseous, my father's body was physically repulsive. It also stank. Years later, I learned from my brother Bob that his casket was not brought inside the church for fear that the seal would burst. Even so, the stench, in the early September heat, was close to overwhelming—which may have been one of the reasons that Ron and I, seven and nine years old at the time, were not permitted to attend the funeral. Even Bob, who was twelve, was discouraged from serving as an altar boy at the funeral Mass, though he managed to persuade my mother otherwise. "Not many people actually went to the cemetery," he once told me. "The smell was so bad that they wanted to get him into the ground as quickly as possible."

This story, related to me sometime in my twenties, lodges in an obscure corner of my brain, where, over time, it develops a nightmarish cast. I try to imagine how my father looked after death. Was his flesh rotten? Did it hang in shreds? In dreams, he comes back to me this way, filling me with fear and disgust.

Our business concluded, the foreman agrees to fill in the fresh grave and dig a new one next to that of my father. "It's really easy these days," he says, "with a backhoe. But I'd better mark this on the map for the front office, and you should check with them before you leave."

As Ron holds out the fax sheet, a flutter of wind blows the paper out of his hand and settles it, disconcertingly, in the open grave. Before our eyes, the foreman jumps in, scoops it up, and hoists himself out again, saying, "It's a good thing they don't dig these things six feet deep anymore."

In a simple, almost comic way, we have solved our dilemma. My mother will have her wish—to be laid to rest next to my father. Ron and I, in our odd, but effective, teamwork, have accomplished this. It's as though we have made a silent pact. Neither of us will be satisfied until we know for certain that her grave will be dug in the right spot.

I am grateful to the foreman for taking our concern seriously. Only afterward am I struck by the oddness of the whole scenario—the debate over headstones and footstones, the probing of the ground, the foreman jumping into the open grave. The point of all this being the indeterminate location of my father's body. Suddenly it dawns on me. We have just settled a question I have been puzzling over since age nine. Once he disappeared, leaving us stranded on a lonely Mississippi sandbar, where did he go? It's as though his story was broken off, interrupted in mid-sentence. I need some way to bring it to a close.

My mother had always insisted that she did not want an open casket. "I don't want a lot of people standing around staring at me," she would say. In our first conversation with the funeral director, Ron and I have to choose. I feel an almost primitive need to view my mother's body but think that Ron might disagree, preferring to honor my mother's wish. "I know she doesn't want to be looked at," I say tentatively, "but I'd like to see her again myself—one last time." "Me too," says Ron, taking me by surprise. "You can have a private viewing for the family," the funeral director suggests, "and then close the casket for the remainder of the visitation." We settle on this compromise.

Given that my mother's casket will be closed for the public part of the visitation, I think it might be a good idea to assemble some photographs, so her friends will have something to look at. I go around the house, gathering what I can find. From the living room, I pick up a studio portrait of my mother, my two brothers, and me from a period in our early childhood. In it, my older brother Bob is about five, I'm around three, and Ron is a baby. My mother must be in her late twenties. She is wearing a V-neck blouse with a pattern of sequins on it, her smooth black hair in the style I remember—parted in the middle and pulled back from her face into an elegant chignon at the nape of her neck. In an upstairs bedroom, I find two photographs from her youth. In one, at about the age of ten, she is seated on the front steps of a house with her parents and mother's sister. Her hair is cut Chinese-style with bangs, and she is wearing a white summer dress. In the other, she is sixteen and just graduated from high school. Her hair is in braids wound around her head in a coronet. With her languid eyes, high cheekbones, and soft skin, she looks older than sixteen. She is seductive and glamorous.

From the upstairs hallway, I gather an 8 × 10 picture of four generations of women, taken by my ex-husband Frank. In it, my mother, my aunt Dorothy, and I are posed in back of my paternal grandmother, who is seated with my four-year-

old daughter Jess on a garden bench. In her fifties now, my
mother is heavier, her hair clipped and permanent-waved,
but she is still beautiful. The last is the photograph of my
parents taken shortly after their marriage that I sent to my
mother for her birthday. After searching all over the house
for it, I finally spy it in the breakfast room, perched on a pile
of magazines, on top of a radiator directly across from the
place where my mother used to sit. Did she ask to have it put
there, I wonder, or is this a random placement?

My brother Ron adds one more picture to this group.
When asked to provide a recent photo to the funeral home to
help the cosmetologist with her makeup, Ron locates a recent snapshot. It looks so spirited and lively that he decides
on the spur of the moment to have it blown up, making copies
for all three of us. He buys a frame, and we take one of these
with us to the funeral home.

We place the pictures on a library table at the back of the
room where my mother's casket is displayed. This room, I
am relieved to see, resembles a chapel, with a domed roof,
stained-glass windows, a cupola with the figure of an angel
pointing upward, and rows of pews. My mother's casket is
placed front and center, where normally an altar would be. I
don't realize until this moment how glad I am that she is not
laid out in a pseudo living room. But I am a little afraid to approach her.

It's 4:00 P.M. of my third day in St. Louis. Jess has arrived
from New York, and though I have told her that I can manage
without her, I am grateful for her presence. I take her hand
and walk down the center aisle toward my mother's casket.
Together, we stand and look at her. The cosmetologist has
done a good job, I think. My mother's mouth looks tense, and
her cheeks are a little flat, but her skin color looks natural,

and her lipstick, a pale pink, is the kind of color she might have worn. Though dead, she is recognizable.

This is not my mother anymore; it's the image of her. But at least she looks like herself. I have brought the thin, white gold wedding ring my father gave her, thinking I might leave it with her. But her hands are interlaced with a rosary and carefully folded, and there is a light veil draped over her body. She looks somehow inviolable—like Snow White, though no lover's kiss can wake her. So I keep the ring on my own finger.

Jess puts her arm around me, and I start to cry. Seeing my mother's body makes me know her death is real. Even the recent photograph of her shows the difference. Peering over her reading glasses with a half smile on her face, she looks sharp and even a little mischievous. The life in her is palpable. Lying in her casket, she is beautiful, but stiff. Although I can't stop looking at her, I know that she is not here.

Gradually, my two brothers, and Bob's daughters Jamie and Christy, join Jess and me at the front of the room. Bob's wife Lois, who is not feeling well, has decided to stay home. The six of us begin to move closer together until we are standing in a line. We put our arms around one another. Some of us are sniffling; some of us are crying. Finally, Ron moves away. He wants to get his camera to take pictures of Mom. This is brave, I think, knowing that I wouldn't have the courage to do this myself.

For a long time, we sit in silence in the front pews. When I am not blowing my nose, I hold Jessica's hand. She, in turn, leans her head against my shoulder the way she did when she was small. I am sorry for everything—for all my resistance to my mother, the years of coldness, the need and rage that kept me from loving her as I feel I do now. I have only one mother, and she is gone.

At last the funeral director tells us it is time to leave the room while they close the casket. They have a policy about not allowing family members to stay, since some become unruly when faced with the finality of this moment. But I see this as just another step in my mother's progress toward her resting place. My aim is to accompany her, not to impede her journey.

Toward the end of the visitation, my mother's caregiver arrives. She is a warm, robust black woman in her seventies, named Mary Dawson. Mary has worked in our household for over thirty years, first as a housekeeper, later as a cook for special occasions and finally as a personal attendant. I have always liked her for her cheerful temper and faith in life, despite the many trials she has experienced. She gives me a firm hug.

"I was worrying about your mama," she says. "She wasn't looking too good on Friday. I just knew she needed help, but she wouldn't hear about my calling the doctor."

I nod and murmur in sympathy. I know what Mary is talking about.

"She was looking forward to you coming for Thanksgiving. And she really liked that present you gave her. She told me to put it right there on the radiator where she can see it. I feel so sad for her, suffering like she did. But her suffering is over now—she's with the Lord."

Mary's conviction awakens mine. Although I can't picture my mother in heaven, I do think of her as relieved of her unhappiness. Seeing her body has brought this home to me. Her spirit—what I want to call her soul—has vanished. It's what all the gospel hymns say; she has been released. I connect this thought with Mary's telling me about the photograph I sent. I am glad to know it was my mother who wanted it placed directly in her line of sight. Did she read my intent? If so, this may be the only time I have managed to cut through our lifelong habit of reserve. With the photograph, I tried to express what I could never have said in words. That in approaching death, I saw her moving toward, rather than away from, her desire.

Jess and I have dinner together, then go back to the house. When we arrive, I find two pieces of paper on the breakfast-room table, with handwritten messages. These are personal statements about my mother by Lois and Jamie to use in the funeral service. Until this moment, I have been in a quandary about the eulogy. Should we have one, or not? I still haven't informed Father Galvin what we plan to do. At one point, I suggest that we might each compose a short statement, which I will weave together into a joint presentation. But Bob and Ron have not felt up to this, and, so far, I've been too busy to think.

Suddenly, I know what to do. I will read Lois's and Jamie's statements and add one of my own. Together, they will speak for all of us. But it's late, and I'm tired, and I want to go to bed. I trust that the words will come to me in the morning.

My mother has a big house, but with all of us here, we're short on beds. Ron suggests that Jess sleep on Mom's hospital bed in the sunroom. I worry about this, thinking that she might be uncomfortable in the bed where Mom died. I tell her that she can sleep with me if she wants, there's plenty of room. "It's OK," she says. "I'll be all right." So we change the sheets and pillowcases and kiss each other good night. In the morning, when I go down to wake her, she tells me she has had the most beautiful dream.

"Do you remember it?" I ask.

"No," she says. "Only that it made me feel really good."

All weekend, I have been hearing the voices of my brother and my mother's friends expressing their sorrow. I begin to notice a couple of refrains and decide to build these into my eulogy. I want to say something truthful about her, and I also want to be kind. She did her best to hold our family together, I think. That was her achievement. The essential privacy of her nature—which I found so frustrating—was something she couldn't help and couldn't change.

I spend a few minutes alone in my mother's bedroom, drafting a brief statement, which I intend to read on behalf of myself and my two brothers. I try to keep it simple and to stick to what I know. Quickly, I write:

> Our mother was a woman of deep strength and courage.
> She had much suffering in her life, which she bore with
> great dignity.
> She never let us down.
> She was very beautiful—in her spirit and in her
> person—and she was a great lady.
> She loved us as we loved her. We will miss her for the
> rest of our lives.

When the time comes, I ask Jess to stand next to me at the pulpit. Even so, I am so overwhelmed that I can barely speak.

The weather has been sunny and unseasonably warm, but the morning of my mother's funeral, it is cool, cloudy, and rainy—just the kind of weather you would expect for such an occasion. The trip to the funeral home and ride in the hearse to the church go by in a blur. My mother's casket is on the move, another step closer to her destination. "Not much farther to go," I murmur to myself. "Don't worry, we'll get you there."

Immaculate Conception church, a gray limestone, neo-Gothic structure, looks just the way it did when I was a child. But the neighborhood around it has deteriorated. Highway 44, completed in the early sixties—one of the first interstates in the country—bisected the parish, dividing middle from working class and white from black populations. The parish now struggles to survive.

A handful of relatives and friends are there to greet us. Jess and I walk down the aisle to the front pew on the right, where I can watch for Father Galvin's signals about when to read. I forget, however, that I don't know anymore when to stand, when to kneel, when to sit, and feel awkward about my ignorance. It doesn't matter, I tell myself. Even though I am an indifferent Catholic, I have as much right to be here as anyone else.

I rise to give the first reading from the Book of Wisdom. It is a lovely passage, which begins, "The souls of the just are in the hands of God, and no torment shall touch them." How much I want to believe this—despite my inability to resurrect my childhood faith in heaven. The reading continues, "Chastised a little, they shall be greatly blessed, because God tried them and found them worthy of himself. As gold in the furnace, he proved them, and as sacrificial offerings he took them to himself." Surely my mother has been tried in her lifetime, proving her mettle by now, her spirit refined into gold. "In the time of their visitation they shall shine and shall dart about as sparks through stubble," I read. "Those who trust in him shall understand truth, and the faithful shall abide with him in love: Because grace and mercy are with his holy ones, and his care is with his elect." I don't know about the elect, but I do believe in grace and mercy. And I do—too late for me to convey this directly to my mother—believe in love.

All of a sudden, the service is over, and I am walking down the aisle behind my mother's casket, gripping Jessica's hand and trying not to lose control.

At the cemetery, there are even fewer mourners—just our family, the priest, one of my mother's long-term neighbors, and my childhood friend, her daughter. The grave, I notice with satisfaction, is now in the right place, though my father's stone is covered with an artificial grass blanket. I push it aside later so that Bob, too, can see where he lies. Father Galvin says a prayer followed by the "Our Father," and then it's over. By now, it is raining, though not heavily. I notice that the gingko tree on the hillside, which just a few days ago stood in autumn glory, has now dropped most of its golden, fan-shaped leaves. They lie, like ancient burnished coins, on the ground, sticking to the soles of my shoes as I walk back to the hearse. I pull them off and tuck a couple of them into the pages of my missal.

When I arrive home in Minneapolis, I place the small wedding photograph of my parents on the desk in my study where I can look at it as I write. They are standing in front of the chapel where they have just been married in the abbreviated ceremony reserved for converts. It is late August, but my father is wearing what looks like a wool tweed suit. My mother, too, is wearing a suit, a slinky outfit with a lynx fur lapel. Their clothes, though elegant, are also practical. No tux for my father, no long white gown or bridal veil for my mother. These are dress clothes that can be used for other occasions. It is the Depression, and my father is just starting in the business of manufacturing seismographs that will take him as far as Hawaii, Australia, and New Zealand. As if to acknowledge the gravity of the occasion, my parents gaze straight at the camera, clear-eyed, but unsmiling.

I take a primitive comfort in this photograph, the moment of their sacramental union standing for their final reunion. I don't mean this literally. I don't believe in the resurrection of the body—not in any corporeal sense. How ludicrous and appalling that would be—my father's decomposed forty-two-year-old corpse joined with my mother's eighty-two-year-old one. Yet I can't help thinking that they are together, like Heathcliff and Cathy in *Wuthering Heights*. Neither could be fully at rest without the other.

Now that my mother lies next to my father, I no longer worry over his ghost. He is anchored by her presence, lying quietly beside her. The thought of his body no longer frightens or disgusts me. Now that my mother's long mourning is over, she feels restored to me, more like the mother I once had, the one who wrote a loving postcard to me and my two brothers.

I have the slides from my parents' trip to Hawaii made into prints. Unlike the snapshots of my parents' wedding, these are color photographs. Slipping them out of their shiny white folder, I am startled by their vividness. These images are almost fifty years old, yet they seem as fresh and immediate as if they had been taken yesterday. In them, my parents look relaxed and happy.

Some of the photos have a blue-green tone, which gives them a timeless, dreamlike quality. In these, my dad is wearing a Hawaiian shirt with a bird-of-paradise print, while my mother is dressed demurely in a white shirred blouse and dark skirt. Both are sporting woven palm hats with fronds spiking out of their wide brims. My father has a silly grin on his face, which makes him look a little goofy, while my mother is half-smiling.

This is how I remember them—not as solemn newlyweds, but as a couple grown comfortable with each other, my mother leaning against my father's shoulder, each with an arm around the other's waist. I can't get enough of looking at them, these two people in whose hands I placed my entire

happiness as a child—the sun and moon of my small universe. It is easy for me to idealize this moment. But gazing at
these photographs, I feel sure of my parents' love for each
other and just as sure that this love flowed out to embrace me
and my two brothers, their eager and trusting children.

The other photograph holds a different set of meanings
for me. This one is brighter, and the color tones seem right,
except for an area of overexposure on one side—fiery fingers
of light that reach toward my parents without touching
them. They are both in Hawaiian dress, my mother in a
fitted, ankle-length muumuu with cream-colored flowers
against an orange background, my father in a red shirt with
a wild yellow and blue design. Both are wearing their palm-
frond hats and have several layers of leis around their necks.
They are standing directly in front of a bush of blooming hibiscus, smiling into the sun, each holding a ripe pineapple in
one outstretched hand.

I choose this moment to accompany my parents into their
afterlife. Already they seem to be in paradise, bedecked in
flowers, backed by a sapphire blue sky and red hibiscus,
holding pineapples, like symbols of abundance. A serendipi-
tous moment captured on film, which I discovered only after
their deaths—speaking to me from some indeterminate place
beyond the grave.

It's only a picture and not even a perfect one, with the orange discoloration on one side. But for me it is a true gift. Some
days, when I look at it, I take comfort in the thought that
both of my parents are at peace. Other days, I feel a sense of
satisfaction that they are together at last. At times, I am even
convinced that they are watching over me, offering me the
kind of benevolent protection they could not provide in life.

Months later, I come to the following realization. The process of organizing my mother's funeral and locating her

gravesite has helped me come to terms with the finality of my father's death. As a child I had never really been sure that he was dead. If so, where was his body? Laying my mother's body to rest has offered me a tangible resolution of this issue. It has also given me the opportunity to grieve for him in a way that I was not allowed to grieve when he died—by participating, step by step, in the unfolding of an ordinary funeral. At each moment, I knew what I was doing and what I was feeling. I no longer had a need to experience my emotions at a safe remove—onscreen and through the image of someone else's pain. Far from being morbid, this experience has opened a new set of possibilities.

For the first time in my life, I take pleasure in the awareness that my parents were once happy, the evidence for which I find in the pictures my mother saved (and hid) in her bedroom vanity. These photographs and slides complement the images from our family home movies. Now that both of my parents are gone, I rediscover them in my own best memory.

My experience of crying at the movies attests to a story I cannot literally recall. Instead of a story, I have the image or shadow of one, which nonetheless bears the weight of my emotional truth. On such shadowy ground, I base my understanding of my past, as well as my faith in life yet to come.

Notes

Home Movies

My thinking about trauma was brought into focus by a weekend seminar organized in the Fall of 1999 by the New Directions in Psychoanalytic Thinking Program, sponsored by the Washington Psychoanalytic Institute and Foundation. The quotation from Cathy Caruth is from *Unclaimed Experience: Trauma, Narrative, History* (Baltimore: Johns Hopkins University Press, 1996). I have also been influenced by the work of Judith Herman and Bessel A. Van Der Kolk. See Herman's *Trauma and Recovery* (New York: HarperCollins, 1992) and Van Der Kolk's edited volume *Traumatic Stress* (New York: Guilford Press, 1996).

House of Cards

I am grateful to Michael Lessac for providing me with an earlier version of the screenplay for *House of Cards* and for allowing me to interview him about the process of transforming this script into the finished film.

The line from *Hamlet* is spoken by Hamlet in his first soliloquy, where he gives expression to his despair over his mother's seeming indifference to his father's memory, as evidenced by her hasty marriage to his uncle. The quotation is from the *Riverside Shakespeare*, ed. G. Blakemore Evans (Boston: Houghton Mifflin, 1974).

"Spring and Fall" is quoted from *The Norton Anthology of Poetry*, ed. Arthur M. Eastman (New York: W.W. Norton & Co., Inc., 1970).

The Piano

Film dialogue quoted in this chapter, along with the comment by the director of photography Stuart Dryburgh, are from Campion's screenplay of *The Piano* (Hyperion: New York, 1993).

Freud speculates on the relationship between Eros and the death instinct in his essay "Beyond the Pleasure Principle." See *The Standard Edition of the Complete Psychological Works of Sigmund Freud,* Trans. James Strachey et. al., ed. James Strachey (London: Hogarth, 1974), 18: 1–64.

Lines from Thomas Hood's poem are quoted from *The Poetical Works of Thomas Hood* (New York: Hurst & Co.).

Fearless

The interview with Peter Weir, conducted by Virginia Campbell, is in *Movieline* magazine, September 1993. See also reviews by David Ansen in *Newsweek,* October 18, 1993; Gary Michael Doult, in *Eye Weekly,* October 21, 1993; Sam McDowell, in the *L.A. Village Voice,* October 15–21, 1993; and Terrence Rafferty in the *New Yorker,* October 25, 1993.

Quotations from St. Augustine's *Confessions* are from the translation by Maria Boulding, O.S.B. (Hyde Park, New York: New City Press, 1997).

The reference to Lacan's concept of the mirror stage is from his essay of the same title in *Écrits: A Selection,* Trans. Alan Sheridan (London: Tavistock, 1977).

Shadowlands

The statistic regarding the incidence of orphanhood in the U.S. is taken from *The Loss That Is Forever,* by Maxine Harris (New York: Penguin, 1995). This book, more than any other, helped me to see how my adult life had been shaped by my failure in childhood to mourn my father's death.

I have used the following books in my references and citations to the work of C.S. Lewis: *A Grief Observed* (New York: Bantam Books, 1976); *The Lion, The Witch and The Wardrobe* (New York: HarperCollins, 1994); *The Magician's Nephew* (New York: Collier

Books, 1970); *The Problem of Pain* (New York: Touchstone, 1996); and *Surprised by Joy* (New York: Harcourt Brace & Co., 1955). Biographical information is drawn from *C. S. Lewis: A Biography,* by A. N. Wilson (New York: Fawcett Columbine, 1990).

Melanie Klein writes about the necessity of rebuilding one's inner world as part of the work of mourning in her essay "Mourning and Manic-Depressive States." See *The Selected Melanie Klein,* ed. Juliet Mitchell (Middlesex, England: Penguin Books, 1986).

Quotations from Rainer Maria Rilke's *Letters to a Young Poet* are from the Stephen Mitchell translation (New York: Random House, 1984).

The etymological background of the word "sad" is taken from the *Oxford English Dictionary* (Glasgow: Oxford University Press, 1971).

The reference to Chaucer's use of the word "sad" is from "Boece," Chaucer's translation of Boethius's *The Consolation of Philosophy.* See *The Works of Geoffrey Chaucer,* ed. F. N. Robinson (Boston: Houghton Mifflin, 1957). I was guided to this reference by the O.E.D.

Blue

Van den Budenmayer is a pseudonym for the composer of the film, Zbigniew Preisner, with whom Kieślowski collaborated on several of his films.

Quotations from Shakespeare's *Twelfth Night* and *The Tempest* are from the *Riverside Shakespeare,* ed. G. Blakemore Evans (Boston: Houghton Mifflin, 1974).

Acknowledgments

WRITING IS A SOLITARY ACTIVITY, but no book is written in isolation. I have been fortunate in the amount of support I have received from friends, writing groups, and institutions over the period of years it took me to complete this memoir. In its earliest stages—before I knew it was a book or even how to organize it—several friends gave me encouragement in the form of nurturing conversation. I am particularly grateful to Janet Adelman, Wendy Martin, and Victoria Nelson for providing a context in which I could begin to formulate my thoughts. At a later stage, I had the opportunity to present portions of the manuscript to various groups, where I received generous and insightful commentary. I benefited especially from the help of the Psychobiography Group at the University of California, Berkeley; the New Directions Program in Psychoanalytic Thinking, sponsored by the Washington Psychoanalytic Institute and Foundation; and the Creative Nonfiction Program at the Loft Literary Center in Minneapolis.

The University of Minnesota provided me with the precious commodity of time in the form of a sabbatical year, a single semester leave and appointment to the Fesler-Lampert Chair in the Humanities. The Fesler-Lampert Chair also subsidized travel and other expenses related to the book, including the extremely able assistance of my graduate Research Assistant Reshmi Dutt.

One of the unusual features of this book is that significant portions of it were written in other people's houses—which functioned for me as a series of private writing retreats. Elizabeth Abel, David Allswang, Gayle Greene, Claire Kahane, and Brenda Webster all lent me the comfort of their homes—

for weeks and even months at a time— where I felt physically and spiritually sheltered.

Many people read the manuscript in full and gave me the benefit of their expert advice. For their patience with a rough manuscript as well as their thoughtful responses, I thank David Allswang, Martha Evans, Marilyn Fabe, Carol Gilligan, Gayle Greene, Mardi Louisell, Josip Novakovich, and Brenda Webster. Marilyn, who shared her own work on film with me over the course of the book's development, was a keen and enthusiastic reader from the beginning. In its later stages, I exchanged work-in-progress with Carol, Gayle, Mardi, and Brenda, the example of whose own memoir writing enlarged and enriched my perspective. Josip gave me the extraordinary gift of line editing. Many of the improvements I made in revising the manuscript are due to his astute reading. I am also grateful to Fiona McCrae, Anne Czarniecki, and Daniel Kos for their understanding of the book and suggestions for further refinement. For the book's remaining defects I am, of course, solely responsible.

I have made particular demands on three people, each of whom has responded with thoughtfulness and compassion. I owe an incalculable debt of gratitude to Dr. Ilse Jawetz, whose calm presence and wise counsel have sustained me for more years than either she or I imagined would be necessary. To my ex-husband Frank, I offer deep thanks for his willingness to re-engage with our mutually painful history by reading this manuscript. My gratitude to my daughter Jessica for her beauty of spirit and generosity of heart is beyond measure. It is she who wakened me to an awareness of the perils and rewards of love, and it is her way of being in the world that enlightens me still.

MADELON SPRENGNETHER is Professor of English at the University of Minnesota, where she teaches critical and creative writing. She has edited several books of literary criticism and is the author of *The Spectral Mother: Freud, Feminism and Psychoanalysis*. Her books of poetry and nonfiction include *The Normal Heart; Rivers, Stories, Houses, Dreams; La Belle et La Bête;* and the co-edited collection *The House on Via Gombito: Writing by North American Women Abroad*. Her book of poems, *The Normal Heart*, was a Minnesota Voices Competition winner. In addition, she has received awards from the Bush Foundation, the Loft Literary Center, and the National Endowment for the Arts. She lives in Minneapolis, where she sees lots of movies.

The text of *Crying at the Movies* has been set in Apollo, a typeface designed by Adrian Frutiger in 1962.

Book design by Wendy Holdman.
Typeset by Stanton Publication Services, Inc.
Manufactured by Friesens on acid-free paper.

Graywolf Press is a not-for-profit, independent press. The books we publish include poetry, literary fiction, essays, and cultural criticism. We are less interested in best-sellers than in talented writers who display a freshness of voice coupled with a distinct vision. We believe these are the very qualities essential to shape a vital and diverse culture.

Thankfully, many of our readers feel the same way. They have shown this through their desire to buy books by Graywolf writers; they have told us this themselves through their e-mail notes and at author events; and they have reinforced their commitment by contributing financial support, in small amounts and in large amounts, and joining the "Friends of Graywolf."

If you enjoyed this book and wish to learn more about Graywolf Press, we invite you to ask your bookseller or librarian about further Graywolf titles; or to contact us for a free catalog; or to visit our award-winning web site that features information about our forthcoming books.

We would also like to invite you to consider joining the hundreds of individuals who are already "Friends of Graywolf" by contributing to our membership program. Individual donations of any size are significant to us: they tell us that you believe that the kind of publishing we do *matters*. Our web site gives you many more details about the benefits you will enjoy as a "Friend of Graywolf"; but if you do not have online access, we urge you to contact us for a copy of our membership brochure.

www.graywolfpress.org

Graywolf Press
2402 University Avenue, Suite 203
Saint Paul, MN 55114
Phone: (651) 641-0077
Fax: (651) 641-0036
E-mail: wolves@graywolfpress.org

Other Graywolf titles you might enjoy are:

Nola: A Memoir of Faith, Art, and Madness
by Robin Hemley

By Herself: Women Reclaim Poetry,
edited by Molly McQuade

A Postcard Memoir
by Lawrence Sutin

Graywolf Forum Four / The Private I:
Privacy in a Public World,
edited by Molly Peacock

Celebrities in Disgrace
by Elizabeth Searle

And Give You Peace
by Jessica Treadway